WHITE ANCESTORS, BLACK SCRIPTURE

The Economy of Human Life &
THE ANCIENT TEXT THAT WASN'T

By Dennis Logan

2025

WHITE ANCESTORS, BLACK SCRIPTURE

The Economy of Human Life & The Ancient Text That Wasn't
By Dennis Logan
With Facsimile Reproduction of *The Economy of Human Life* (1751)

Introduction, Commentary, and Appendices by Dennis Logan

© 2025 Penemue Media, LLC
All rights reserved.

This work contains material originally published in 1751 and now in the public domain.
This edition—including its introduction, editorial preface, commentary, comparative charts, appendices, typesetting, formatting, and additional scholarly material—is copyrighted by Penemue Media, LLC.

No part of this edition may be reproduced, stored in a retrieval system, or transmitted in any form or by any means—electronic, mechanical, photocopying, recording, or otherwise—without prior written permission of the publisher, except in the case of brief quotations used in critical articles or reviews.

Editor: Dennis Logan
Publisher: Penemue Media
ISBN: 978-1-964297-25-5
Printed in the United States of America
First Penemue Media Edition: 2025
Cover Design: Penemue Media
Interior Layout & Modern Typesetting: Dennis Logan

DEDICATION

To our ancestors—named and unnamed, recorded and forgotten—
who made miracles out of whatever scraps the world allowed them.

To those who kept dignity alive with borrowed texts, broken histories,
oral fragments, and the small flames of hope they guarded in their hands.

To the elders still living, and to the children rising now,
who continue the work with the same courage, the same vision,
and the same determination to make meaning out of the incomplete.

This book is for you.

May we **take what they left**
— *truths, errors, fragments, inventions*—
and **shape them into something** *wiser, cleaner, and more whole*
than *anything* they had the *TIME* or *FREEDOM* to **BUILD**.

What they **preserved** in *pieces,*
may we **restore** in *understanding.*

What they *endured in silence,*
may we *speak with grace.*

PREFACE

On Lineage, Inheritance, and the Healing of a Family Tree

This volume is born from a simple but delicate premise: that wisdom does not diminish when we tell the truth about its origins. If anything, it grows stronger. *The Economy of Human Life* has lived many lives—first as an eighteenth-century English moral treatise, then as an "Oriental" manuscript, later as a Rosicrucian lesson, and finally as one of the quiet tributaries feeding the spiritual imagination of Black America in the early twentieth century. Each transformation tells a story not of deception, but of longing: a longing for dignity, antiquity, identity, and spiritual grounding in a world that did not always offer those things freely.

This preface exists to gently prepare the reader for a conversation that may touch tender places. For many in our American spiritual family—Moorish Americans, Black Muslims, Rosicrucians, seekers shaped by New Thought, students of metaphysics—the texts included here are not merely books; they are vessels of identity, memory, and cultural healing. The purpose of this edition is *not* to undermine that sacred work, but to honor it more completely by understanding how these texts traveled, who shaped them, and how they became meaningful to communities that needed them most.

We include in these pages a full facsimile of Robert Dodsley's **Economy of Human Life**, so the reader may see the text in its earliest form—before it was asked to wear the robes of Brahmin, Tibetan, or esoteric master. Alongside it, we offer carefully chosen excerpts from the **Circle Seven Koran**, a brilliant and uniquely American creation that braided together scripture, allegory, and metaphysics with a visionary hand. These two texts, rarely placed side by side, illuminate how ideas migrate and evolve: one born in Enlightenment London, the other in the creative crucible of Black Chicago under Jim Crow.

Many of the historical threads woven through this study touch sensitive ground. They involve misunderstandings and misattributions, yes—but also adaptation, resilience, and genuine spiritual genius. Our intention is not to "debunk" but to **contextualize**, not to embarrass but to **clarify**, not to fracture but to **heal**. Every movement touched by these texts—Moorish Science, the early Nation of Islam, Rosicrucian orders, and numerous Black fraternal and metaphysical traditions—played a vital role in shaping the moral and spiritual landscape of America. They deserve respect, not reduction.

This work is offered with deep compassion for our elders and ancestors, who pursued wisdom with the tools available to them in their time. They did not have the internet, digitized archives, or instantaneous cross-cultural scholarship. They had intuition, community, and an unyielding hunger for truth. That hunger carried them far—often farther than the texts themselves intended to go.

What we hope to provide here is a fuller map of the journey: a genealogy of how certain writings crossed oceans, languages, publishing houses, and racial boundaries; how they were renamed, repurposed, and reborn; and how they came to live in our Black American spiritual bloodstream. This is not an exposé. It is an act of transparency made possible by the tools of 2025—an offering meant to bring us closer to one another, not farther apart.

If America is a family tree, then the spiritual lineages explored here are branches that grew in different directions, sometimes unaware of their shared root systems. This edition asks us to look at those roots together, with humility and gratitude. By doing so, we honor every hand—white, Black, mystic, scholarly—that carried these ideas forward. And we acknowledge that the story of how wisdom is used is often more important than where it began.

My hope is that this edition serves as a bridge: between scholarship and devotion, between history and identity, between what was inherited and what can now be understood. May these pages illuminate, not unsettle; clarify, not condemn; and ultimately strengthen the shared lineage that binds us across time, culture, and experience.

— **Dennis Logan**
The Honorable Scribe
Richmond, VA 2025

PART I — ORIGINS OF A MISUNDERSTOOD TEXT

How an English moral pamphlet became an "Eastern scripture"

The World of Robert Dodsley (1740s England)

The story of *The Economy of Human Life* opens not in an Eastern monastery or a desert shrine but in the heart of eighteenth-century London, at a moment when literature, philosophy, and print capitalism were beginning to reshape the intellectual world. Robert Dodsley emerged from the margins of society—first as a footman, then as a poet, and finally as one of Britain's most respected publishers. His rise was unusual for the period. Literary London was dominated by class hierarchy, yet Dodsley navigated it with instinctive skill, building networks among writers, editors, and thinkers who trusted him to bring their manuscripts into public life. His shop on Pall Mall became a meeting point for the century's most ambitious minds: Samuel Johnson, Alexander Pope, Edmund Burke, and the broad constellation of Enlightenment figures who believed ideas could elevate both individuals and society.

It was within this vibrant world of salons and pamphlets, encyclopedias and moral treatises, that Dodsley composed *The Economy of Human Life*—a work designed to offer ethical instruction in the elegant, aphoristic style fashionable at the time. Anonymous publication was not unusual for moral literature. Anonymity allowed the work to stand on its own merit; it also protected authors from criticism in a period when every opinion invited rebuttal. But Dodsley employed another layer of distance: he framed the text as if it were drawn from a Brahmin manuscript, a relic of ancient India rendered into English for the benefit of Western readers. This gesture was part of a broader Enlightenment fascination with "Eastern" wisdom—the idea that faraway civilizations possessed moral clarity that Europe had lost in its political and religious quarrels.

To modern readers, this may appear deceptive. In its own era, it was a stylistic convention. Eastern sages had become literary archetypes, not unlike the trope of the "noble Roman" in earlier centuries. They embodied timelessness, simplicity, and virtue. By writing through this imagined voice, Dodsley was not claiming secret knowledge but participating in a widespread cultural habit: presenting universal truths in a foreign idiom so that readers would receive them with a sense of distance and awe. The affect worked. The book circulated widely, and its readers accepted both its tone and its disguise as part of the genre. Few were troubled by the fiction because the fiction was transparent.

The "Oriental Composition" Disguise

The pretense of Eastern authorship did not last long. By 1800, just a half-century after its release, the publisher openly admitted that the original "disguise of an Oriental composition" had been removed, noting that the author's identity was already known. The text no longer needed the mask. It had been recognized for what it was: an English moral work written in a poetic style meant to evoke antiquity. Readers of that era understood that the Brahmin framing was a literary flourish rather than an actual translation. The confession was brief, almost casual, because the audience was familiar with such devices. Within the circles that still read Dodsley, there was no mystery left.

And yet, the mask did not die. It simply went dormant. Once the work fell out of fashion in Britain, its contextual footnotes faded from memory. Later printers reissued the text without the editorial explanation. New readers encountered only the maxims and the stately prose. Its origins—clear to eighteenth-century audiences—were obscured by time, reprints, and the Atlantic crossing. When the text resurfaced in America a century later, its readers encountered it without the benefit of the original admissions. The Enlightenment joke had become, over time, an unintended mythology.

This fragile chain of transmission explains how *The Economy of Human Life* reentered public consciousness not as a known eighteenth-century work but as a fragment of ancient Eastern philosophy. By the early twentieth century, the elaborate disclaimers printed in early British editions were no longer part of the book's life. Only the aura remained.

European "Eastern Wisdom" as a Genre

Dodsley's text must also be situated within a larger literary pattern. Throughout the seventeenth and eighteenth centuries, European writers produced a stream of "translations" attributed to Chinese sages, Egyptian priests, and Chaldean astrologers. Most were not direct translations at all. They were European compositions written in a style meant to approximate—or romanticize—foreign antiquity. *The Morals of Confucius*, for example, presented Confucian ethics through a distinctly European moral lens. Works claiming to reveal "Egyptian mysteries" often drew more from Greek Neoplatonism than from anything preserved on papyrus. Even the "Chaldean Oracles," popular among scholars, were later shown to be products of much later philosophical speculation.

These texts were shaped by the same impulse that guided Dodsley: the belief that universal truths traveled more easily when attributed to distant civilizations unburdened by Europe's religious and political divisions. Enlightenment readers found reassurance in wisdom that seemed to predate Christianity and monarchy alike. The "East" served as a symbolic terrain—idealized, abstracted, and safely removed from contemporary disputes. Writers leaned into this aesthetic because it allowed ethical maxims to appear timeless, and publishers embraced it because it sold.

This genre set the stage for something the original authors could not foresee. Once these pseudo-Eastern works left the salons of Europe and entered broader circulation—crossing oceans, entering colonial spaces, filtering through missionary libraries, and eventually being repackaged by occult publishers—their fictional frames lost their context. They traveled farther than their disclaimers. They reached readers for whom the imagined antiquity felt authentic, not theatrical.

By the time *The Economy of Human Life* arrived in the hands of early twentieth-century mystics and mail-order occultists, it was no longer understood as an Enlightenment artifact. It had become a freestanding piece of "timeless wisdom," a perfect candidate for reinvention. What had once been a literary device in London could now be adopted as genuine scripture by communities searching for origins outside of Western religious authority.

This was the soil in which the text would begin its second life—a life shaped not by Dodsley's intentions, but by the needs and imaginations of those who encountered it in a world far removed from eighteenth-century England.

PART II — THE OCCULT RESURRECTION (1900–1930)

How Chicago and California turned Dodsley into a mystical master

L.W. de Laurence and the Birth of American Occult Publishing

By the turn of the twentieth century, *The Economy of Human Life* had nearly vanished from mainstream British reading culture. Its Enlightenment context faded, its anonymity forgotten, and its earlier disclaimers locked in editions no longer widely available. Yet a new environment was forming in America—one defined by mass printing, mail-order mysticism, and a hunger for spiritual instruction outside the traditional church. Chicago became the unlikely capital of this esoteric marketplace, a city where immigration, industrialization, and religious experimentation created a unique demand for practical magic, spiritual healing, and accessible wisdom literature. It was here that L.W. de Laurence built his empire.

De Laurence was not a scholar in the academic sense; he was an entrepreneur who recognized that spiritual aspiration could travel by post. His catalog contained spellbooks, talismans, manuals of ceremonial magic, dream interpreters, and cheaply printed classics of occultism. The business model was simple: take forgotten nineteenth-century translations, expired copyrights, and esoteric curiosities—then repackage them as ancient, authoritative, and indispensable. Chicago's printing industry made this possible. With cheap labor and rising literacy, publishers could flood the country with small paperbacks that promised empowerment, protection, and self-mastery to anyone willing to send a dollar.

It was in this context that *The Economy of Human Life* re-emerged under a new title: *Infinite Wisdom* (1923). De Laurence did what London readers of 1800 knew better than to do—he revived the original mask. The work was presented not as an eighteenth-century English treatise but as a Tibetan manuscript translated by "Dr. Cao-Tsou," a name invented to restore the exotic distance that had once been a literary flourish. In a catalog full of grimoires, psalmic talismans, and occult manuals, the book fit naturally. De Laurence's audience expected mystical antiquity. He supplied it.

This creative reattribution was part of his broader strategy. He blended Eastern mystique with biblical Egypt, Hindu icons with Solomonic magic, and Indian ascetics with Rosicrucian allegory. His customers—many of them African American, Caribbean, or immigrant readers barred from formal lodges and libraries—encountered these materials as their first exposure to "ancient wisdom" outside the authority of Christianity. What had begun as Enlightenment playacting in England reappeared in Chicago as a spiritual inheritance waiting to be claimed.

H. Spencer Lewis, AMORC, and the Rosicrucian Rebrand

While Chicago was printing its mystical paperbacks, California nurtured its own form of esotericism—shaped by Theosophy, mystic tourism, and the belief that hidden masters guided human civilization from Himalayan sanctuaries. H. Spencer Lewis, founder of AMORC, built his order in this atmosphere. His approach to lineage was aspirational: the Rosicrucians of Europe had not formally commissioned him, but he believed the archetype was real enough to manifest under a new American form. To support this vision, he needed authoritative texts, symbols of antiquity, and literature that carried the tone of timeless guidance.

Thus *Unto Thee I Grant* (1925) was born—a work credited to "Sri Ramatherio," framed as a translation from Tibetan archives discovered by AMORC emissaries. In reality, the core text was Dodsley's treatise once again, filtered through de Laurence's earlier edition and embellished with the imagery of Eastern monastic secrecy. The book included staged photographs of Tibetan libraries, dramatic claims of ascended masters, and hints of a lineage linking AMORC to ancient philosophical schools. Whether these gestures were sincere aspirations or theatrical devices, they served their function: they gave the order a scripture.

Lewis did not plagiarize in the modern legal sense—*The Economy of Human Life* was in the public domain. But he remixed it within a framework that promised esoteric succession. The text's structure made it ideal for this purpose: short maxims, moral guidance, and the appearance of universalism without doctrinal obligations. It was the kind of material a burgeoning mystical order could attach its identity to with ease. As de Laurence had done for his customers, Lewis did for his initiates: he used the aura of Eastern antiquity to lend authority to a spiritual vision still under construction.

Occult Groups Fighting for Legitimacy Through Ancient Lineages

The early twentieth century was filled with new esoteric societies searching for credibility in a crowded landscape. The Theosophical Society claimed Mahatmas in Tibet; the Hermetic Brotherhood of Luxor spoke of Egyptian adepts; Freemasons traced symbolic ancestry to Solomon's Temple; and Rosicrucian-inspired groups looked toward imaginary monasteries beyond the Himalayas. In this environment, ancient texts—real or imagined—became essential. A group with a book sounded older, wiser, and more grounded than a group without one.

Dodsley's text, reborn under various Eastern disguises, became a tool for these movements. It was a perfect candidate: portable, authoritative in tone, thematically universal, and free of Christian dogma. Above all, it was free. The absence of copyright allowed small publishers to adopt it without legal risk, making it a staple of mail-order catalogues and initiatory literature. The book's Enlightenment origins offered practical ethics; its fabricated antiquity offered mythic lineage. Few texts delivered both.

Why Occult Publishers Preferred Public Domain Pseudo-Eastern Texts

The revival of Dodsley's work was not incidental—it was the result of structural forces. After the 1909 Copyright Act, a vast archive of eighteenth- and nineteenth-century literature became openly reproducible. For occult publishers, this was an opportunity. They could reissue old works with new titles, elaborate backstories, and modern typesetting, transforming forgotten British pamphlets into mystical artifacts. These publishers understood something simple: antiquity sells.

A book like *The Economy of Human Life* could be printed cheaply, framed as ancient, and marketed as indispensable spiritual instruction. In the American imagination, especially among communities underserved by mainstream religious institutions, the promise of "ancient wisdom" carried enormous power. The distance between the original text and its new identity widened with each reprint. Print capitalism became a machine that manufactured antiquity faster than scholars could correct it.

By the time the text reached Black American religious innovators in Chicago, Harlem, Detroit, and the broader diaspora, it had already passed through multiple layers of reinvention. Each layer obscured its origin further. And each reinvention prepared it for a final transformation—one that would elevate it into scripture.

PART III — BLACK AMERICA AND THE SEARCH FOR ANCIENT WISDOM

How a repackaged British pamphlet became part of a larger spiritual renaissance

Why Black Communities Were Drawn to Indo-Asian Wisdom

When Dodsley's moral maxims reemerged in America, reshaped by de Laurence and Rosicrucian publishers, they entered a country transformed by race, migration, and the struggle for dignity. For Black Americans living under Jim Crow, Christianity carried both spiritual nourishment and the deep wound of having been weaponized against them. Segregated pews, racist sermons, and the lingering theology of enslavement made many question whether the faith of their oppressors could fully hold their aspirations. This did not produce a rejection of Christianity; rather, it opened a search for complementary or alternative lineages that could restore a sense of antiquity, inheritance, and agency.

In this search, Asia—whether imagined, mythic, or loosely understood—became a symbolic refuge. India, China, and Japan were colonized, exploited, and exoticized by the West, yet they carried ancient civilizations, complex spiritual systems, and cultural pride that seemed untouched by Europe's racial hierarchies. Black Americans recognized a parallel struggle. The Indo-Asian world represented a history older than empire, unbroken by slavery, and rich in spiritual prestige. Many saw in the concept of the "Asiatic" a way to reclaim global belonging: a way to identify as heirs to something older than America's racial categories.

Early Black readers were also encountering Buddhism, Hinduism, and Islam through new translations, traveling lecturers, and the global press. Asian reformers—Tagore, Vivekananda, Okakura, and others—were publishing widely, and their critiques of Western civilization resonated deeply with African Americans seeking new intellectual languages to describe their condition. Thus, when pseudo-Eastern texts circulated through Chicago and Harlem, they were not read as curiosities. They were read as portals into a broader human story.

The Black Esoteric Renaissance (1890–1930)

Between Reconstruction and the Great Depression, Black America experienced a surge of spiritual creativity that rarely receives the scholarly attention it deserves. Rootworkers, spiritualists, conjure doctors, and itinerant prophets shaped local religious life. Black Masonic lodges provided ritual, fraternity, and philosophical grounding. New Thought ministers preached mental mastery and divine possibility to congregations hungry for hope. Pan-African thinkers reimagined Africa not as a place of loss but as a font of ancient wisdom. Egyptology entered sermons and street lectures; Islam, once marginal, began to take on new symbolic meaning; and esoteric Christianity blended with Afro-diasporic traditions in ways that still define Black spirituality today.

The environment was electric: Harlem full of dreambooks and lodges, Chicago alive with metaphysicians and mystics, Detroit steeped in the language of prophecy and rebirth. Black religious life was no longer confined to the Protestant denominational system—it was expanding through bookstores, newspapers, theaters, fraternal halls, and streetcorner debates. New identities were being forged, drawing from anywhere dignity could be found. In this cultural moment, a text claiming Eastern antiquity did not need to prove itself. It needed only to arrive.

Why De Laurence's Catalog Reached Black Homes First

The spread of pseudo-Eastern texts among Black communities was made possible by structural exclusions. White-owned bookstores rarely stocked occult literature, and when they did, they catered to elite European-American audiences. Libraries were segregated, and many Black neighborhoods lacked them entirely. Yet literacy rates in Black America were rising rapidly, and there was a hunger for written guidance—both spiritual and practical—that mainstream institutions did not provide.

Mail-order publishing filled the gap. De Laurence's catalog could travel anywhere a letter carrier was willing to go. Rural households, urban apartments, churches, lodges, barber shops, and beauty parlors became points of distribution. His advertisements appeared in Black newspapers and magazines; his books circulated through word-of-mouth networks and fraternal orders. Caribbean governments eventually banned his catalog out of concern for its influence, which only increased its mystique. Hoodoo practitioners interviewed in the 1920s and 1930s consistently named de Laurence publications as essential tools of their craft. In effect, his catalog became the first Black metaphysical library—unintentionally, but unmistakably.

This is how *The Economy of Human Life*, now wearing Tibetan and Rosicrucian clothing, entered the world of Black religious innovation. By the time it reached these communities, it had passed through three transformations: Enlightenment fiction, occult reinvention, and mail-order mobilization. Yet what mattered most was how it was received. The text's simplicity, moral clarity, and scriptural cadence aligned perfectly with a moment when Black Americans were remaking themselves intellectually, spiritually, and nationally. Its supposed antiquity offered authority; its universalism offered freedom; its anonymity allowed it to be claimed without constraint.

In this environment, Dodsley's voice—translated, disguised, and remixed across two centuries—became part of a much larger story: the story of Black America reclaiming wisdom from any corner of the world in order to imagine a future larger than the one the nation had offered.

PART IV — THE CIRCLE SEVEN KORAN AND THE BIRTH OF NEW SCRIPTURE

How Dodsley → de Laurence → Lewis became Black scripture

Noble Drew Ali and the Circle Seven Koran (1927)

By the time Noble Drew Ali arrived in Chicago, the city had become a spiritual crossroads where competing metaphysical traditions lived side by side. Spiritualist mediums, Theosophists, Black Masons, evangelical storefront preachers, rootworkers, and occult booksellers operated within blocks of one another. It was a place where an ambitious teacher could gather ideas from many shelves—sometimes without knowing who originally wrote them—and weave them into something that spoke directly to the needs of Black people in the 1920s. The Circle Seven Koran emerged from this environment, not as an imitation of any single book but as a creative synthesis built from the texts circulating most widely at the time.

The first half of the Circle Seven closely parallels *The Aquarian Gospel of Jesus the Christ* (1908), a New Thought reimagining of the life of Jesus that moved him freely through India, Egypt, and Tibet. Its cosmology, language of "Christ Consciousness," and imagery of Eastern travels appear almost unchanged. The latter chapters track with *Unto Thee I Grant*—Dodsley's repackaged moral treatise, now bearing de Laurence's and AMORC's Eastern veneers. A few passages echo the tone and metaphysical outlook of *OAHSPE*, especially in their division between higher and lower selves, celestial hierarchies, and the moral language of purification. None of this diminishes Drew Ali's originality; it reveals the world of sources he had access to and the ingenuity with which he repurposed them for Black selfhood.

Why Drew Ali Likely Never Knew the Authors Were White

Nothing in the printed materials available to Ali suggested the texts he used were European. *The Aquarian Gospel* appeared in cheap editions stripped of Levi Dowling's illustrations, which depicted a fair-skinned Jesus but were rarely included in mass-market reprints. *Unto Thee I Grant* claimed Tibetan, Indian, or Rosicrucian origins depending on the publisher. *OAHSPE* was marketed as an angelic revelation rather than the product of a New York dentist's occult experiments. These works arrived in Chicago already clothed in Eastern identity, long after the Enlightenment-era disclaimers had become obscure. To Ali, the materials likely felt authentic within the logic of their own packaging—ancient, Asiatic, non-Christian, and therefore useful for constructing a spiritual identity independent of white American authority.

How the "Egyptian Adept" Fits the de Laurence Archetype

The famous story in Moorish Science Temple lore—that Ali encountered an Egyptian mystic who revealed ancient secrets to him—fits hand-in-glove with the marketing world created by de Laurence and reinforced by AMORC. De Laurence's catalogs were filled with descriptions of unnamed adepts, wandering sages, and keepers of hidden temples who passed suppressed knowledge to worthy initiates. Many were fictional, but they functioned as archetypal figures meant to authorize the books being sold. Whether Ali encountered a person, a story, or simply the idea of such a figure, the trope was everywhere in the mail-order occult world. The "Egyptian Adept" was not a lie—it was the era's defining metaphor for the transmission of esoteric wisdom. Ali simply adopted the idiom of his time and filled it with meaning that served his community.

Circle 7 as a Work of Black Syncretic Genius

The real achievement of the Circle Seven Koran lies not in the originality of its ingredients but in the transformation of those ingredients into a text with new purpose. Ali fused Christian moral philosophy, New Thought metaphysics, pseudo-Brahmin ethics, Theosophical cosmology, and Afro-Asiatic identity into a single scripture that addressed the psychological, political, and cultural needs of Black Americans. The resultant work was neither derivative nor accidental; it was a deliberate act of creative nation-building. By reframing borrowed material as Moorish wisdom, Ali affirmed that Black people had ancient lineage, divine authority, and a place in the world's sacred history. The Circle Seven did what the earlier sources could not: it gave the text back to a people who needed it.

W.D. Fard and the Earliest Nation of Islam Curriculum

When W.D. Fard appeared in Detroit in the early 1930s, he entered a landscape already shaped by the Moorish Science movement, Eastern metaphysics, and Afro-Asiatic identity claims. His earliest teachings—before leading to the structured doctrine of the Nation of Islam—reflected an eclectic mixture of Qur'anic references, numerology, linguistic play, and mythic geography. The Qur'ans circulating among his earliest followers were themselves a study in contrasts. Some were simple Arabic-print imports; others used George Sale's English translation, a heavily Christianized reading framed through 18th-century imperial eyes.

But it was the *Maulvi Muhammad Ali* translation (1917), produced by the Lahore Ahmadiyya movement, that seems to have shaped the early intellectual framework of the NOI. Muhammad Ali's commentary emphasized anti-colonial resistance, universal moral reform, and the intellectual dignity of non-Western peoples. Britain viewed the Lahore Ahmadiyya as politically subversive, and their works were banned or restricted in parts of the empire. For Black Americans confronting segregation and institutionalized racism, such a text offered not only access to Islam but a vocabulary of global critique. It spoke to the same hunger that had drawn earlier readers to Indo-Asian wisdom: the need for a spiritual identity unbound by white authority.

Fard's Afro-Asiatic Language Innovations

Fard's linguistic creativity—his reframing of Black Americans as "Asiatic," his intentional re-mapping of world geography, his emphasis on etymology and symbolic languages—mirrored strategies already visible in Moorish Science. Both movements used Asia not simply as a location but as a conceptual homeland, a place of ancient dignity from which Black people could reclaim a sense of lineage cut short by slavery. This wasn't academic geography; it was cultural psychology. By naming Black Americans "Asiatics," Fard and Ali placed them in a world older than Europe, older than the Atlantic slave trade, and older than America itself. Such reframing created space for new scripture, new nations, and new possibilities.

The Black Re-Creation of Esoteric Asia

Taken together, these movements show how Black innovators re-Africanized and re-humanized texts that began their lives as European inventions of "the East." *The Economy of Human Life* was reborn as *Infinite Wisdom*, then as *Unto Thee I Grant*, and finally as part of the Circle Seven Koran—each stage adding layers of meaning until the text became unrecognizable from its Enlightenment origins. The same pattern would inform the early Nation of Islam, where Islamic texts, Afro-diasporic memory, and esoteric lore fused into a new cosmology. Myth became identity; identity became community; community generated scripture. This was not deception but the dynamic process by which marginalized groups assemble meaning from whatever tools are available.

In that sequence—Economic Life → Infinite Wisdom → Unto Thee I Grant → Circle 7 → NOI—we see the evolution of a British moral treatise into a foundation stone of multiple Black religious movements. Through these reinterpretations, "Asia" became a mirror in which Black America could see its own nobility. The Asiatic Black Man, the Moor, the Lost-Found Muslim—all were attempts to reclaim personhood in a world determined to erase it. This spiritual creativity became a survival technology, an intellectual resistance, and eventually a shared metaphysics that empowered generations.

PART V — ARCHETYPES, FREQUENCY, AND THE "REAL" ANCIENT WISDOM

How myths become true through human consciousness

By the time we reach the modern era, the question is no longer whether *The Economy of Human Life* was "real" Brahmin wisdom or whether its later reincarnations were genuinely Tibetan, Rosicrucian, or Islamic. What matters is why each version felt real enough to inspire discipline, identity, and spiritual transformation. At a certain point in the transmission of knowledge, the genealogy of a text becomes less important than the human need that animated it. Movements grow not because their sources are perfect but because they resonate with something universal—something archetypal, patterned, and profoundly human.

The Archetype of the Hidden Adept

Every tradition has a figure who appears at the margins of recorded history: the sage who travels unseen, the teacher who emerges in times of crisis, the guardian of forgotten knowledge who passes wisdom to those prepared to receive it. Christian Rosenkreuz, the fictional founder of Rosicrucianism, was one version of this. The Sufi Khidr, the Taoist Immortals, the yogic siddhas, the desert monks of early Christianity, the itinerant griots of West Africa—all participate in the same symbolic role. Their historicity varies, but their function is constant: they represent the possibility that knowledge is older and deeper than any institution can claim. The prevalence of this archetype explains why movements like Moorish Science and the early Nation of Islam were not weakened by the questionable origins of their texts; they were strengthened by the familiarity of the mythic role their founders stepped into.

Universal Patterns of Initiation

If the hidden adept is the archetype, the initiate is the universal character who recognizes him. Across cultures—from Sufi lodges to Taoist hermitages, from Masonic halls to Yoruba initiation houses—the qualities associated with "the one who is ready" are remarkably similar: discernment, humility, symbolic literacy, and the willingness to endure transformation. People across different societies recognize each other because the pattern is older than their languages. This explains why Black Americans encountering Orientalist texts in the early twentieth century were able to transform them into authentic spiritual resources. They did not merely copy foreign traditions; they stepped into an archetypal script that had been running globally for millennia.

The Frequency Network: How "Orders" Form Without Founders

Some communities form around charismatic leaders, but others arise almost spontaneously, as if people tuned into the same wavelength without meeting. Contemporary theorists describe this phenomenon with different terms—*morphic resonance, collective unconscious, distributed cognition, noetic fields*—but they all capture the idea that ideas cluster around shared mental or emotional frequencies. Groups of people, often separated by great distance, can arrive at similar beliefs or practices because they are responding to the same psychological or social conditions. In this light, the emergence of Moorish Science, the Nation of Islam, various Afro-Asiatic identity movements, and Black esoteric orders appears less like coincidence and more like a synchronized cultural awakening.

How Ideas Create Communities (Not the Other Way Around)

When examining these movements historically, it is tempting to map their organizational trees, track their founders, and trace their textual borrowings. But a deeper reading shows that the ideas themselves were the primary agents of formation. A concept like "the Asiatic Black man," or "lost-and-found wisdom," or "ancient moral law" creates the community that gathers around it—not the reverse. Ideas with archetypal weight exert gravity. They draw people into orbit and then generate practices, rituals, and identities to sustain themselves. In this sense, texts like *Unto Thee I Grant* or the Circle Seven Koran functioned as nuclei around which communities could condense.

How a Fiction Becomes a Brotherhood

Rosicrucianism began as a literary hoax—a satire aimed at mocking Europe's obsession with secret societies. Yet because the ideas contained within the satire were archetypally compelling, people began forming real groups in response. Over the centuries, those groups acquired practices, teachings, initiation rituals, and lineages that were entirely genuine, even though their origin was not. The same process unfolded in Black America: texts whose origins were fictional, misattributed, or misunderstood nevertheless became catalysts for new religious and cultural formations. Their "truth" was measured not by their authors but by their effect.

The Self-Fulfilling Prophecy of Esoteric Myth

When a community believes it has inherited ancient wisdom, it behaves as if that wisdom is real—and the behavior makes it real in practice. This is the paradox at the heart of all esoteric traditions. A myth, when lived with sincerity and discipline, becomes a mechanism for self-transformation. It organizes thought, reshapes identity, and produces real spiritual outcomes. In this view, the impact of *The Economy of Human Life* on Moorish Science and the Nation of Islam is entirely understandable. The text may have begun as English moral philosophy, but once adapted by new custodians, it became part of a living tradition of survival, self-definition, and metaphysical empowerment.

Parallel Dynamics in Moorish Science and Early NOI

Both communities inherited texts already framed as "Eastern wisdom." Both reinterpreted that material through the lens of Black experience. Both transformed myth into identity and identity into nationhood. And both demonstrate how a people cut off from ancestral memory can build new genealogies using whatever fragments are available. Far from being naïve borrowers of white occultism, these movements exemplified a uniquely African American capacity to repurpose, reframe, and re-enchant inherited materials into something more powerful than their source.

PART VI — A NEW READING OF *THE ECONOMY OF HUMAN LIFE* (2025)

Reissuing the text with honesty, respect, and historical understanding

By 2025, we stand in a moment where nearly every piece of inherited wisdom is being reexamined, often for the first time with the tools and access required to understand its full history. The digital age has not only given us unprecedented access to ancient sources—it has also exposed the creative misattributions, pious frauds, intentional mythmaking, and accidental genealogies that shaped the spiritual texts of the last three centuries. In this climate, *The Economy of Human Life* reemerges not as the "ancient Brahmin scripture" it once claimed to be, nor as the Tibetan or Rosicrucian teaching later publishers fashioned from it, but as something more compelling: a case study in how wisdom travels, how communities transform what they inherit, and how texts accumulate power as they cross cultural boundaries.

This book has been many things in its long journey—an Enlightenment moral essay, an Orientalist curiosity, an occult manual, a Rosicrucian lesson, a Moorish Science teaching, and, indirectly, part of the soil from which the early Nation of Islam drew intellectual nutrients. Each phase was shaped by the needs and imaginations of the communities who used the text. That migration is what gives the work its modern significance. When we reissue it today, we are not simply restoring an eighteenth-century artifact; we are honoring the historical truth of how diverse peoples—white, Black, mystic, rationalist, oppressed, and hopeful—found something usable in the same cluster of aphorisms.

Why This Book Matters in 2025

The twenty-first century has brought a renewed hunger for "ancient wisdom," but also a heightened sensitivity to cultural appropriation, authenticity, and historical accuracy. Paradoxically, misinformation has never spread faster, nor has the desire for lineage ever been more intense. In this landscape, honesty becomes a necessary virtue. *The Economy of Human Life* matters not because of its supposed antiquity, but because of its documented influence on movements that shaped the intellectual and spiritual lives of millions of African Americans. The text stands as evidence of a deeper truth: authentic spiritual transformation can emerge from sources far more humble, hybrid, and human than the myths surrounding them admit.

The renewed interest in Afro-Asiatic identity, in tracing diaspora lineages, and in confronting the distortions of colonial scholarship makes this book a timely example of how ideas change hands without losing their power. It also demonstrates how Black religious innovators reinterpreted, re-energized, and re-spiritualized texts that earlier publishers used primarily as marketing curiosities. For modern readers, this history offers both caution and inspiration: caution against uncritical reception, and inspiration in seeing how communities can transform borrowed ideas into instruments of liberation.

How Modern Readers Must Approach Inherited "Scriptures"

A twenty-first century reader cannot simply accept the prefaces and lineages that accompanied earlier editions. Instead, we are invited to approach this work with a mental toolkit that did not exist in the eighteenth or early twentieth century: awareness of Orientalism, familiarity with colonial-era pseudotranslations, understanding of Theosophical syncretism, and sensitivity to how marginalized communities adopt and adapt ideas to meet their needs. This does not diminish the spiritual value these groups found in the text; if anything, understanding the chain of transformation allows us to appreciate their creativity and resilience more fully.

Reading this book honestly in 2025 means holding two truths at once: that *The Economy of Human Life* was not an ancient Asiatic manuscript, and also that its later interpreters—especially in Black America—made it function like one. A modern reader must learn to differentiate between authorship and stewardship, between origin and impact, between the literal history of a text and the lived history it helped produce. That distinction opens the door to a more mature and liberating mode of spiritual literacy.

A Text That Traveled Through Many Hands

What makes this book worthy of renewed study is not the originality of its content, but the astonishing breadth of its cultural journey. Few other eighteenth-century pamphlets traveled so widely, changed names so often, or influenced such distinct movements. From Enlightenment London, where Dodsley crafted it as a moral essay framed with an exotic veneer; to Chicago's occult presses, where L.W. de Laurence refashioned it as Tibetan metaphysics; to California's Rosicrucian prints, where H. Spencer Lewis placed it within a lineage of esoteric masters; to the temples and homes of Black America, where it was read alongside the *Circle Seven Koran*, the *Aquarian Gospel*, the *OAHSPE*, and the early Qur'anic teachings circulating within the Nation of Islam—this text passed through worlds that rarely speak to each other in academic history.

Because of that journey, *The Economy of Human Life* sits at the crossroads of multiple traditions: Enlightenment humanism, Orientalist fantasy, American occultism, Afro-Asiatic identity formation, Black Masonic culture, and the earliest formulations of Black Islamic theology. To tell this story honestly is to reveal a hidden cultural map stretching across three centuries and four continents.

What We Gain by Telling the Truth

Restoring the real history of this text does not weaken it. Instead, it gives us deeper insight into how wisdom circulates and evolves. It allows us to credit the imagination and ingenuity of Black religious pioneers who transformed Euro-American spiritual leftovers into engines of self-knowledge and dignity. It helps us recognize how texts can be reborn in new hands, shaped by new needs, and animated by new horizons of meaning. This clarity does not undermine the power of the book—it highlights the creative labor that made it meaningful.

What we gain, ultimately, is respect: respect for the communities who made something sacred out of borrowed fragments, respect for the complexity of spiritual transmission, and respect for the human capacity to turn imperfect sources into transformative guidance. By tracing the journey of *The Economy of Human Life* from its Enlightenment cradle to its role in Black esoteric history, we honor both the text and the people who gave it life long after its original context faded.

PART VII — CLOSING MEDITATION: WHO OWNS WISDOM?

As we reach the end of this long journey—from Enlightenment London to Chicago print shops, from California mystic lodges to Black temples and living rooms—we inevitably return to a question that has haunted every page of this genealogy: **who owns wisdom?** We have traced how a European moral pamphlet disguised itself as Eastern scripture; how occult publishers repackaged it to serve their own lineages; how Black Americans, facing the cruelties of Jim Crow and the constraints of white Christianity, repurposed those same words into instruments of pride, dignity, and metaphysical self-discovery. At each turn, the same text meant something different because the people who held it needed different things. And in that simple observation lies the heart of our closing meditation.

Ancient Wisdom Is Not About Who Wrote It, But Who Used It

A people do not adopt a text because its origin is perfect; they adopt it because its spirit is useful. The authorship of *The Economy of Human Life*—whether known, hidden, or mythologized—never fully determined its destiny. What mattered was the imagination of those who read it. When Black Americans encountered this text in the early twentieth century, they were not looking for academic exactness; they were searching for a vocabulary of dignity beyond the limits imposed by the society around them. If a text claimed Asiatic ancestry, that was not a deception but a possibility—a window into an older lineage that colonial systems had long denied them. The truth of the text was measured not by its factual origin but by the dignity it conferred and the discipline it inspired.

How Communities Remake Texts

Every religious tradition, ancient or modern, is built on reinterpretation. Communities create the meaning they need from whatever fragments history leaves them. Christians fashioned a universal ethic from a Jewish apocalyptic movement. Sufis transformed legalist Islam into a mystical pathway. Taoists stitched together folk religion, poetry, and political philosophy into a flowing cosmic doctrine. Black Americans, faced with the twin challenges of displacement and oppression, did what all great civilizations have done: they took the materials available and remade them into something new, coherent, and powerful.

In this light, *The Economy of Human Life* became more than the sum of its misattributions. It became a canvas onto which multiple communities projected their highest longings. Instead of asking whether those projections were "correct," we should ask what those communities achieved through their reinterpretations.

How Creation Myths Empower

Myths do not lose their potency when their origins are examined; they lose their potency when their meaning is forgotten. Every spiritual lineage crafts a story about where its wisdom comes from—not because the story must be literally true, but because the story situates the community within the cosmos. Creation myths give people the courage to live with purpose. This is as true for a Rosicrucian initiate as it is for a Moorish American, a Black Muslim in the 1930s, or a young seeker today who feels the weight of navigating a fractured world.

The stories surrounding this text—Brahmin manuscripts, Tibetan masters, Egyptian adepts—were never merely marketing inventions. They were attempts to bind moral teaching to antiquity, to say: *this wisdom is older and larger than any one nation's power.* For Black Americans, this claim had an added resonance: it allowed them to reimagine themselves as participants in a global sacred continuum rather than as subjects of a racialized hierarchy.

The Difference Between Authorship and Custodianship

Authorship is a historical fact. Custodianship is a moral act. What *The Economy of Human Life* became in Black America was not determined by Dodsley or de Laurence or H. Spencer Lewis. It was determined by the Black readers who took it seriously, integrated it into their worldview, and placed it alongside other writings—scriptural, apocryphal, and aspirational—that helped them navigate a world that rarely acknowledged their humanity. In that sense, the Black custodians of this text did something more profound than any earlier publisher: they made the text **ethical**, **living**, and **communal**.

What Black America Did With This Book Was More Important Than Where It Came From

If there is one truth this entire genealogy displays, it is this: the transformative power of a text comes not from its origin but from its adoption. The genius of Black esoteric innovators was not in discovering ancient manuscripts but in transforming the spiritual debris of a globalizing world into pathways of self-knowledge and liberation. They wove together texts that academics might dismiss, but they infused them with meaning that no academic apparatus could ever fully measure.

To tell this story honestly is not to diminish their work—it is to honor the extraordinary intellectual creativity that allowed our elders and ancestors to build something sacred from the fragments they were given.

The Transformation Matters More Than the Origin

Every text, no matter how exalted, is a vessel awaiting a reader. Origins matter for scholarship; transformations matter for life. In the case of this book, the transformation stands as testimony to a wider historical truth: Black communities in America turned borrowed texts into blueprints for survival. They turned pseudo-Eastern pamphlets into scripture, reinterpreted colonial translations into liberation theology, and used the idea of an Asiatic heritage to imagine themselves beyond the limits of American racial identity.

That transformation is the real ancient wisdom—not because it is old, but because it is deeply human.

Reclaiming, Reinterpreting, and Moving Forward

To revisit this text in 2025 is not to expose a fraud; it is to illuminate a lineage. It is to say that hidden within misattributions and misdirections lies a record of our collective effort to locate wisdom wherever it could be found. It is to commit ourselves to new transparency without abandoning the reverence our elders had for the tools that sustained them. It is to acknowledge how far we have come and how much more there is to uncover.

New scholarship can deepen our understanding. New transparency can restore trust. New generations can continue the work with clearer eyes. But the heart of the matter remains unchanged: wisdom does not belong to a single culture, race, or author. It belongs to the people who use it well.

Why 2025 Is the Perfect Year to Revisit This History

Because we finally have the tools, the freedom, and the collective maturity to tell this story whole. Because our generation stands at a threshold where the collapse of false authority can give birth to more grounded forms of truth. And because reconnecting with this lineage—honestly, clearly, and without shame—allows us to build spiritual futures that neither deny nor depend upon the myths of the past.

In that spirit, this reissue is not simply a restoration; it is an invitation. To read wisely. To remember generously. And to carry forward the wisdom our predecessors cultivated, not by pretending it was ancient, but by proving it is enduring.

THE
ECONOMY
OF
HUMAN LIFE.

IN TWO BOOKS.

BY ROBERT DODSLEY.

WITH

SIX ELEGANT ENGRAVINGS BY MACKENZIE,

FROM DESIGNS BY CRAIG AND UWINS.

LONDON:

Printed for Sherwood, Neely, and Jones; F. C. and J. Rivingtons; Longman, Hurst, Rees, and Orme; J. Harris; Cuthell and Martin; B. Crosby and Co.; R. Scholey; C. Brown; and T. Hughes.

1809.

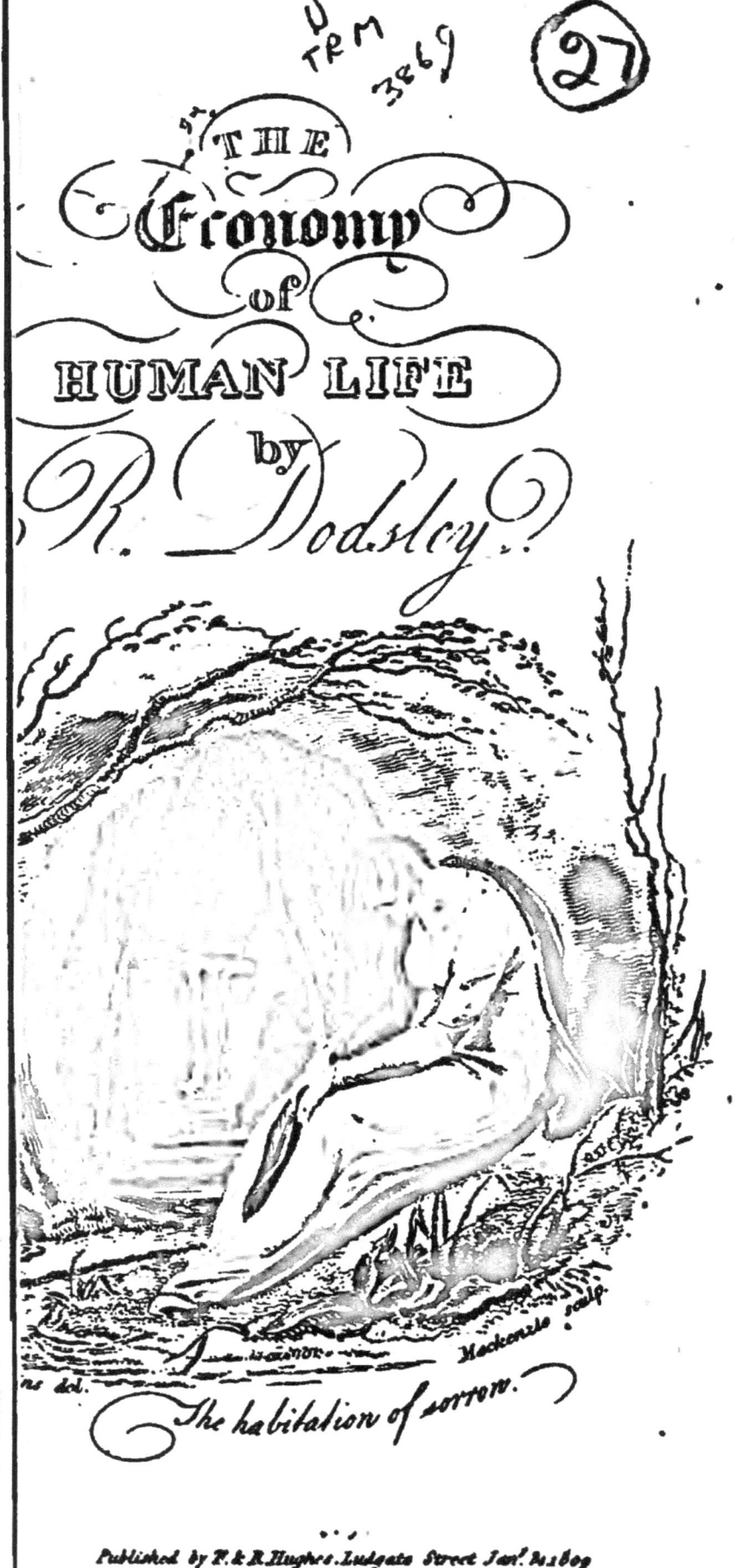

The habitation of sorrow.

ADVERTISEMENT.

THE deserved esteem in which this little work has been held for a series of years, the excellence of its moral principles, the concise but forcible style in which it inculcates the precepts of virtue, justice, benevolence, and piety, and which renders it so pleasing and easy a vehicle of instruction to youth, preclude the necessity of any apology for the present improved edition of the ECONOMY OF HUMAN LIFE. As a work admirably designed for the improvement of youth, the publishers have been anxious to render it, in point of typographical neatness and elegance of embellishments, superior to any edition that has yet appeared; and they doubt not but that the designs, which are by Craig and Uwins, and engraved by Mackenzie, will give general satisfaction. The only liberty taken with the original has been to omit the disguise of an oriental composition, which the modesty of the author first gave to his work, but which now was considered as unnecessary; the real name of the author having long been known to the public.

MEMOIRS

OF

MR. ROBERT DODSLEY.

MEMOIRS

OF

Mr. ROBERT DODSLEY,

AMONG the many blessings which the people of this country are in the enjoyment of in a pre-eminent degree beyond those of most other nations, one of the most pleasing and striking is, that merit and abilities in the lowest station, when accompanied by virtue, integrity, and perseverance in their possessor, rarely fail to raise a man, however humble his origin, to honourable distinction and independence. He who to talents joins industry and diligence in his pursuits need never dispair of improving his condition; but without those virtues the most splendid endowments are frequently illusory. The subject of the following biographical sketch is a striking example of the truth of these observations.

ROBERT DODSLEY, the ingenious author of the Economy of Human Life, was born at Mansfield, in Nottinghamshire, in the year 1703. His parents, being persons in a humble situation of life, were unable to give him more than a common education; so that, as he himself informs us, he was unacquainted with the learned languages, and consequently destitute of those aids, which by many are supposed necessary to the formation of a correct and elegant taste, though of such a taste there appears not the slightest deficiency in his works.

His first setting out in life was in the humble capacity of a footman, in the family of the Honourable Mrs. Lowther; but by a happy incident his talents soon raised him from this low station. Having composed a dramatic piece called the "Toy-shop," and that piece being shewn to Mr. Pope, then in the zenith of his reputation, and justly regarded as the arbiter of of English literature, the delicacy of its satire, though clothed with the greatest simplicity of design, so strongly recommended the author to the notice of that celebrated poet, that he continued from that time to the day of his death a warm and a zealous friend to Mr. Dodsley; and though he had no particular connection with the theatres, yet procured him such an interest as insured his piece being brought immediately on the stage, where it met with the success it merited; as did also a farce, intitled " the King, and Miller of Mansfield," on the plan of the "*Parti de Chasse de Henri IV.*" which made its appearance in the ensuing year, viz. 1736, and which in the present season (1809) has been revived in an Italian dress at the King's theatre in the Haymarket.

The success of these pieces having put Mr. Dodsley into possession of a sum of money considerable for one in his circumstances of life, he wisely determined not to trust to the Muses alone for his future support, but with the capital he had so honourably gained entered into the business of a bookseller. In this station, the recommendations of Mr. Pope, and his own merit, soon obtained him not only the countenance of persons of the first ability, but also of those of the first rank, and in a few years raised him to great eminence in his profession, of which he was almost, if not altogether, at the head. But neither his success in trade, nor the increase of his reputation as a writer, had any effect in changing the disposition of this amiable and excellent man. In his prosperity he was mindful of the early encouragement which his own talents had met with, and ever ready to give the same opportunity of advancement to those of others; and he ever spoke of his literary labours with that modesty which is inseparable from true genius. It is difficult whether we ought most to applaud the humility of his character, which he preserved when raised to the most affluent circumstances, or the grateful remembrance he retained, and ever expressed, to the memory of those to whom he owed the obligation of his first being taken notice of in life.

As a writer, there is an ease and elegance which runs through the whole of Mr. Dodsley's works, which is oftentimes more pleasing than a more laboured and ornamented manner; and this high praise is due to him, that he always wrote on the side of virtue and good morals. In verse his numbers are flowing, if not sublime, and his subjects constantly well chosen and entertaining. In prose he is familiar, yet chaste; and in his dramatic pieces he has ever kept in his eye the one great principle, *delectando pariterque monendo*; some general moral is constantly conveyed in the general plan, and particular instruction dispersed in the particular strokes of satire.

Mr. Dodsley wrote six dramatic pieces; and besides these he published, in his life time, a little collection of his works in one volume 8vo, under the modest title of "Trifles," and a poem of considerable length, intitled "Public Virtue." A second volume of his works was collected after his decease, consisting of, 1. Cleone; 2. Melpomene, or the Region of Terror and Pity, an Ode; 3. Agriculture, a poem; 4. the Economy of Human Life. Having acquired a very handsome fortune by his profession, Mr. Dodsley retired from business some years before his death, which happened on the 23d of September, 1764, at the house of his friend, the reverend Mr Spence, at Durham. His remains were interred in the Abbey Churchyard, at Durham, and the following inscription was placed on a tombstone erected to his memory on the spot.

If you have any Respect
for uncommon Industry and Merit,
regard this Place!
in which are interred the Remains
of
MR. ROBERT DODSLEY;

Who, as an Author, rais'd himself
much above what could have been expected
from one in his Rank in Life,
and without learned Education;
And who, as a Man, was scarce
exceeded by any in Integrity of Heart
and Purity of Manners and Conversation.
He left this Life for a better,
September 23, 1764, in the 61st Year of his
Age.

In the preface to the collection of "Old Plays," which bears his name, and which was republished after his death, there is the following testimony to his character, evidently from the pen of one who was well acquainted with his worth, and with it we shall conclude our account of this excellent person. "The first edition of the present volumes was one of the many plans produced by the late Mr. Robert Dodsley, a man to whom literature is under so many obligations, that it would be unpardonable to neglect this opportunity of informing those who may have received any pleasure from the work, that they owe it to a person whose merit and abilities raised him from an obscure situation in life to affluence and independence. Modest, sensible, and humane, he retained the virtues which first brought him into notice after he had attained wealth sufficient for every wish which could arise from the possession of it. He was a generous friend, an encourager of men of genius, and acquired the esteem and respect of all who were acquainted with him. It was his happiness to pass the greater part of his life with those whose names will be revered by posterity; by most of whom he was loved as much for the virtues of his heart, as he was admired on account of his excellent writings."

CONTENTS.

Memoirs of the AUTHOR — — Page v

Introduction — — — — 5

PART I.
DUTIES THAT RELATE TO MAN, CONSIDERED AS AN INDIVIDUAL.

Sect.
I. Consideration — — — 11
II. Modesty — — — 13
III. Application — — — 15
IV. Emulation — — — 18
V. Prudence — — — 20
VI. Fortitude — — — 23
VII. Contentment — — — 25
VIII. Temperance — — — 27

PART II.
THE PASSIONS.

I. Hope and Fear — — — 32
II. Joy and Grief — — — 34

Sect. Page.
III. Anger - - - 37
IV. Pity - - - 40
V. Desire and Love - - - 42

PART III.
WOMAN.

I. Woman - - - 46

PART IV.
CONSANGUINITY; OR, NATURAL RELATIONS.

I. Husband - - - - 52
II. Father - - - 55
III. Son - - - - 57
IV. Brothers - - - 59

PART V.
PROVIDENCE; OR, THE ACCIDENTAL DIFFERENCES IN MEN.

I. Wise and Ignorant - 62
II. Rich and Poor - - 64
III. Masters and Servants - 67
IV. Magistrates and Subjects 69

PART VI.
THE SOCIAL DUTIES.

I. Benevolence - - 74
II. Justice - - - 76

Sect.		Page.
III. Charity		78
IV. Gratitude		80
V. Sincerity		82

PART VII.
RELIGION.

I. Religion		86

BOOK II.

PART I.

MAN, CONSIDERED IN THE GENERAL.

I. Of the Human Frame and Structure	92
II. Of the Use of the Senses	95
III. The Soul of Man; its Origin and Affections	98
IV. Of the Period and Uses of Human Life	103

PART II.

MAN, CONSIDERED IN REGARD TO HIS INFIRMITIES, AND THEIR EFFECTS.

I. Vanity	110
II. Inconstancy	114
III. Weakness	119

Sect.		Page
IV.	Of the Insufficiency of Knowledge	123
V.	Misery	128
VI.	Of Judgment	132
VII.	Presumption	137

PART III.

OF THE AFFECTIONS OF MAN WHICH ARE HURTFUL TO HIMSELF AND OTHERS.

I.	Covetousness	145
II.	Profusion	149
III.	Revenge	151
IV.	Cruelty, Hatred, and Envy	156
V.	Heaviness of Heart	160

PART IV.

OF THE ADVANTAGES MAN MAY ACQUIRE OVER HIS FELLOW-CREATURES.

I.	Nobility and Honour	169
II.	Science and Learning	174

PART V.

OF NATURAL ACCIDENTS.

I.	Prosperity and Adversity	181
II.	Pain and Sickness	185
III.	Death	187

THE ECONOMY OF HUMAN LIFE.

INTRODUCTION.

Bow down your heads unto the dust, O ye inhabitants of earth! be silent and receive, with reverence, instruction from on high.

Wheresoever the sun doth shine, wheresoever the wind doth blow, wheresoever there is an ear to hear, and a mind to conceive; there let the precepts of life be made known, let the maxims of truth be honoured and obeyed.

All things proceed from God. His power is unbounded, his wisdom is from eternity, and his goodness endureth for ever.

He sitteth on his throne in the centre, and the breath of his mouth giveth life to the world.

He toucheth the stars with his finger, and they run their course rejoicing.

On the wings of the wind he walketh abroad, and performeth his will through all the regions of unlimited space.

Order, and grace, and bounty, spring from his hand.

The voice of wisdom speaketh in all his works; but the human understanding comprehendeth it not.

The shadow of knowledge passeth over the mind of man as a dream; he seeth as in the dark; he reasoneth, and is often deceived.

But the wisdom of God is as the light of heaven; he reasoneth not; his mind is the fountain of truth.

Justice and mercy wait before his throne; benevolence and love enlighten his countenance for ever.

Who is like unto the Lord in glory? Who in power shall contend with the Almighty? Hath he any equal in wisdom? Can any in goodness be compared unto him?

He it is, O man! who hath created thee: thy station on earth is fixed by his appointment: the powers of thy mind are the gift of his goodness: the wonders of thy frame are the work of his hand.

Hear then his voice, for it is gracious; and he that obeyeth, shall establish his soul in peace.

PART I.

DUTIES THAT RELATE TO MAN,

CONSIDERED AS AN INDIVIDUAL.

SECTION I.

CONSIDERATION.

Commune with thyself, O man, and consider wherefore thou wast made.

Contemplate thy powers, thy wants, and thy connections; so shalt thou discover the duties of life, and be directed in all thy ways. Proceed not to speak or to act before thou hast weighed thy words, and examined the tendency of every step thou shalt take; so shall disgrace fly far from thee, and in thy house shall shame be a stranger: repentance shall not visit thee, nor sorrow dwell upon thy cheek.

The thoughtless man bridleth not his tongue; he speaketh at random, and is entangled in the foolishness of his own words.

As one that runneth in haste, and leapeth over a fence, may fall into a pit on the other side, which he doth not see; so is the man that plungeth suddenly into any action, before he hath considered the consequences thereof.

Hearken therefore unto the voice of Consideration; her words are the words of wisdom, and her paths shall lead thee to truth and safety.

SECTION II.

MODESTY.

Who art thou, O man, that presumest on thine own wisdom? or why dost thou vaunt thyself on thine own acquirements? The first step towards being wise, is to know that thou art ignorant; and if thou wouldst not be esteemed foolish in the judgment of others, cast off the folly of being wise in thine own conceit.

As a plain garment best adorneth a beautiful woman, so a decent behaviour is the greatest ornament of wisdom.

The speech of a modest man giveth lustre to truth, and the diffidence of his words absolveth his error.

He relieth not on his own wisdom; he weigheth the counsels of a friend, and receiveth the benefit thereof.

He turneth away his ear from his own praise, and believeth it not; he is the last in discovering his own perfections.

Yet, as a veil addeth to beauty, so are his virtues set off by the shade which his modesty casteth upon them.

But, behold the vain man, and observe the arrogant; he clotheth himself in rich attire, he walketh in the public street, he casteth round his eyes, and courteth observation.

He tosseth up his head, and overlooketh the poor; he treateth his inferiors with insolence, and his superiors in return look down on his pride and folly with laughter.

He despiseth the judgment of others, he relieth on his own opinion, and is confounded.

He is puffed up with the vanity of his imagination: his delight is to hear and to speak of himself all the day long.

He swalloweth with greediness his own praise, and the flatterer in return eateth him up.

THE VAIN MAN.

SECTION III.

APPLICATION.

Since the days that are past are gone for ever, and those that are to come, may not come to thee, it behoveth thee, O man, to employ the present time, without regretting the loss of that which is past, or too much depending on that which is to come.

This instant is thine, the next is in the womb of futurity, and thou knowest not what it may bring forth.

Whatsoever thou resolvest to do, do it quickly; defer not till the evening what the morning may accomplish.

Idleness is the parent of want and of pain; but the labour of virtue bringeth forth pleasure.

The hand of diligence defeateth want; prosperity and success are the industrious man's attendants.

Who is he that hath acquired wealth, that hath risen to power, that hath clothed himself with honour, that is spoken of in the city with praise, and that standeth before the king in his counsel? Even he that hath shut out Idleness from his house; and hath said unto Sloth, Thou art mine enemy.

He riseth up early, and lieth down late; he exerciseth his mind with contemplation, and his body with action, and preserveth the health of both.

The slothful man is a burden to himself, his hours hang heavy on his head: he loitereth about, and knoweth not what he would do.

His days pass away like the shadow of a cloud, and he leaveth behind him no mark for remembrance.

His body is diseased for want of exercise; he wisheth for action, but hath not power to move; his mind is in darkness; his thoughts are confused; he longeth for knowledge, but hath no application. He would eat of the almond, but hateth the trouble of breaking its shell.

His house is in disorder, his servants are wasteful and riotous, and he runneth on towards ruin: he seeth it with his eyes, he heareth it with his ears, he shaketh his head and wisheth, but hath no resolution; till ruin cometh upon him like a whirlwind, and shame and repentance descend with him to the grave.

SECTION IV.

EMULATION.

If thy soul thirsteth for honour, if thy ear hath any pleasure in the voice of praise, raise thyself from the dust whereof thou art made, and exalt thy aim to something that is praiseworthy.

The oak that now spreadeth its branches towards the heavens, was once but an acorn in the bowels of the earth.

Endeavour to be first in thy calling, whatever it be; neither let any one go before thee in well-doing: nevertheless, do not envy the merits of another, but improve thine own talents.

Scorn also to depress thy competitor by dishonest or unworthy methods: strive to raise thyself above him only by excelling him; so shall thy contest for superiority be crowned with honour, if not with success.

By a virtuous emulation the spirit of a man

is exalted within him; he panteth after fame, and rejoiceth as a racer to run his course.

He riseth like the palm-tree in spite of oppression; and as an eagle in the firmament of heaven, he soareth aloft, and fixeth his eye upon the glories of the sun.

The examples of eminent men are in his visions by night; and his delight is to follow them all the day long.

He formeth great designs, he rejoiceth in the execution thereof, and his name goeth forth to the ends of the world. But the heart of the envious man is gall and bitterness; his tongue spitteth venom; the success of his neighbour breaketh his rest.

He sitteth in his cell repining, and the good that happeneth to another, is to him an evil.

Hatred and malice feed upon his heart, and there is no rest in him.

He endeavours to depreciate those that excel him, and putteth an evil interpretation on all their doings.

He lieth on the watch, and meditates mischief: but the detestation of man pursueth him, and he is crushed as a spider in his own web.

SECTION V.

PRUDENCE.

Hear the words of Prudence, give heed unto her counsels, and store them in thine heart: her maxims are universal, and all the virtues lean upon her: she is the guide and mistress of human life.

Put a bridle on thy tongue: set a guard before thy lips, lest the words of thine own mouth destroy thy peace.

Let him that scoffeth at the lame, take care that he halt not himself: whosoever speaketh of another's failings with pleasure, shall hear of his own with bitterness of heart.

Of much speaking cometh repentance, but in silence is safety.

A talkative man is a nuisance to society; the ear is sick of his babbling, the torrent of his words overwhelmeth conversation

Boast not of thyself, for it shall bring contempt upon thee; neither deride another, for it is dangerous.

A bitter jest is the poison of friendship; and he that cannot restrain his tongue, shall have trouble.

Furnish thyself with the proper accommodations belonging to thy condition: yet spend not to the utmost of what thou canst afford, that the providence of thy youth may be a comfort to thy old age.

Let thine own business engage thy attention; leave the care of the state to the governors thereof.

Let not thy recreations be expensive, lest the pain of purchasing them exceed the pleasure thou hast in their enjoyment.

Neither let prosperity put out the eyes of circumspection, nor abundance cut off the hands of frugality; he that too much indulgeth in the superfluities of life, shall live to lament the want of its necessaries.

From the experience of others, do thou learn wisdom; and from their failings correct thine own faults.

When thou hast proved a man to be honest, lock him up in thine heart as a treasure; regard him as a jewel of inestimable price.

Refuse the favours of a mercenary man;

they will be a snare unto thee; thou shalt never be quit of the obligation.

Use not to-day what to-morrow may want; neither leave that to hazard which foresight may provide for or care prevent.

Yet expect not even from prudence infallible success; for the day knoweth not what the night may bring forth.

The fool is not always unfortunate, nor the wise man always successful; yet never had a fool a thorough enjoyment: never was a wise man wholly unhappy.

SECTION VI.

FORTITUDE.

Perils, and misfortunes, and want, and pain, and injury, are more or less the certain lot of every man that cometh into the world.

It behoveth thee, therefore, O child of calamity! early to fortify thy mind with courage and patience, that thou mayest support, with a becoming resolution, thy allotted portion of human evil.

As the camel beareth labour, and heat, and hunger, and thirst, through deserts of sand, and fainteth not; so the fortitude of man shall sustain him through all perils.

A man of a noble spirit disdaineth the malice of fortune; his greatness of soul is not to be cast down.

He hath not suffered his happiness to depend on her smiles, and therefore with her frowns he shall not be dismayed.

As a rock on the sea-shore, he standeth firm, and the dashing of the waves disturbeth him not.

He raiseth his head like a tower on a hill, and the arrows of fortune drop at his feet.

In the instant of danger the courage of his heart sustaineth him; and the steadiness of his mind beareth him out.

He meeteth the evils of life as a man that goeth forth into battle, and returneth with victory in his hand.

Under the pressure of misfortunes, his calmness alleviates their weight, and his constancy shall surmount them.

But the dastardly spirit of a timorous man betrayeth him to shame.

As a reed is shaken with a breath of air, so the shadow of evil maketh him tremble.

In the hour of danger he is embarrassed and confounded; in the day of misfortune he sinketh, and despair overwhelmeth his soul.

SECTION VII.

CONTENTMENT.

Forget not, O man! that thy station on earth is appointed by the wisdom of the Eternal; who knoweth thy heart, who seeth the vanity of all thy wishes, and who often, in mercy, denieth thy requests.

Yet for all reasonable desires, for all honest endeavours, his benevolence hath established, in the nature of things, a probability of success.

The uneasiness thou feelest, the misfortunes thou bewailest, behold the root from whence they spring! even thine own folly, thine own pride, thine own distempered fancy.

Murmur not therefore at the dispensations of God, but correct thine own heart: neither say within thyself, " If I had wealth, or power, or leisure, I should be happy;" for know, they all bring to their several possessors their peculiar inconveniences.

The poor man seeth not the vexations and anxieties of the rich, he feeleth not the difficulties and perplexities of power, neither knoweth he the wearisomeness of leisure; and therefore it is that he repineth at his own lot.

But envy not the appearance of happiness in any man, for thou knowest not his secret griefs.

To be satisfied with a little is the greatest wisdom; and he that increaseth his riches, increaseth his cares: but a contented mind is a hidden treasure, and trouble findeth it not.

Yet if thou sufferest not the allurements of fortune to rob thee of justice, or temperance, or charity, or modesty, even riches themselves, shall not make thee unhappy.

But hence shalt thou learn, that the cup of felicity, pure and unmixed, is by no means a draught for mortal man.

Virtue is the race which God hath set him to run, and happiness the goal, which none can arrive at till he hath finished his course, and received his crown in the mansions of eternity.

SECTION VIII.

TEMPERANCE.

The nearest approach thou canst make to happiness on this side the grave, is to enjoy from heaven understanding and health.

These blessings, if thou possessest, and wouldst preserve to old age, avoid the allurements of Voluptuousness, and fly from her temptations.

When she spreadeth her delicacies on the board, when her wine sparkleth in the cup, when she smileth upon thee, and pursuadeth thee to be joyful and happy; then is the hour of danger, then let Reason stand firmly on her guard.

For if thou hearkenest unto the words of her adversary, thou art deceived and betrayed.

The joy which she promiseth, changeth to madness, and her enjoyments lead on to diseases and death.

Look round her board; cast thine eyes upon her guests, and observe those who have been allured by her smiles, who have listened to her temptations.

Are they not meagre or bloated? are they not sickly? are they not spiritless.

Their short hours of jollity and riot are followed by tedious days of pain and dejection. She hath debauched and palled their appetites, that they have no relish for their nicest dainties: her votaries are become her victims; the just and natural consequence which God hath ordained, in the constitution of things, for the punishment of those who abuse his gifts.

But who is she that with graceful steps, and with a lively air, trips over yonder plain?

The rose blusheth on her cheeks, the sweetness of the morning breatheth from her lips; joy, tempered with innocence and modesty, sparkleth in her eyes, and from the cheerfulness of her heart she singeth as she walks.

Her name is Health; she is the daughter of Exercise and Temperance; their sons inhabit the mountains of the northern regions.

They are brave, active, and lively, and partake of all the beauties and virtues of their sister.

Vigour stringeth their nerves, strength dwelleth in their bones, and labour is their delight all the day long.

The employments of their father excite their appetites, and the repasts of their mother refresh them.

To combat the passions is their delight; to conquer evil habits their glory.

Their pleasures are moderate, and therefore they endure; their repose is short, but sound and undisturbed.

Their blood is pure, their minds are serene, and the physician findeth not the way to their habitations.

But safety dwelleth not with the sons of men, neither is security found within their gates.

Behold them exposed to new dangers from without, while a traitor within lurketh to betray them.

Their health, their strength, their beauty and activity, have raised desire in the bosom of lascivious love.

She standeth in her bower, she courteth their regard, she spreadeth her temptations.

Her limbs are soft and delicate; her attire is loose and inviting. Wantonness speaketh in her eyes, and on her bosom sits Temptation. She beckoneth them with her finger, she wooeth them with her looks, and by the smoothness of her tongue, she endeavoureth to deceive.

Ah! fly from her allurements, stop thy ears to her enchanting words. If thou meetest the languishing of her eyes; if thou hearest the softness of her voice; if she casteth her arms about thee, she bindeth thee in chains for ever.

Shame followeth, and disease, and want, and care, and repentance.

Enfeebled by dalliance, with luxury pampered, and softened by sloath, strength shall forsake thy limbs, and health thy constitution; thy days shall be few, and those inglorious; thy griefs shall be many, yet meet with no compassion.

PART II.

THE PASSIONS.

SECTION I.

HOPE AND FEAR.

The promises of hope are sweeter than roses in the bud, and far more flattering to expectation; but the threatenings of fear are a terror to the heart.

Nevertheless, let not hope allure, nor fear deter thee from doing that which is right; so shalt thou be prepared to meet all events with an equal mind.

The terrors even of death are no terrors to the good; he that committeth no evil hath nothing to fear.

In all thy undertakings let a reasonable assurance animate thy endeavours; if thou despairest of success, thou shalt not succeed.

Terrify not thy soul with vain fears, neither let thy heart sink within thee from the phantoms of imagination.

From fear proceedeth misfortune; but he that hopeth, helpeth himself.

As the ostrich, when pursued, hideth his head, but forgetteth his body; so the fears of a coward expose him to danger.

If thou believest a thing impossible, thy despondency shall make it so; but he that persevereth, shall overcome all difficulties.

A vain hope flattereth the heart of a fool; but he that is wise pursueth it not.

In all thy desires let reason go along with thee, and fix not thy hopes beyond the bounds of probability; so shall success attend thy undertakings, thy heart shall not be vexed with disappointments.

SECTION II.

JOY AND GRIEF.

Let not thy mirth be so extravagant as to intoxicate thy mind, nor thy sorrows so heavy as to depress thy heart. This world affordeth no good so transporting, nor inflicteth any evil so severe, as should raise thee far above, or sink thee much beneath, the balance of moderation.

Lo! yonder standeth the house of joy. It is painted on the outside, and looketh gay; thou mayest know it from the continual noise of mirth and exultation that issueth from it.

The mistress standeth at the door, and calleth aloud to all that pass by; she singeth and shouteth, and laugheth without ceasing.

She inviteth them to go in and taste the pleasures of life, which she telleth them are nowhere to be found but beneath her roof.

But enter not thou into her gate; neither associate thyself with those who frequent her house.

They call themselves the sons of joy; they laugh and seem delighted: but madness and folly are in all their doings.

They are linked with mischief hand in hand, and their steps lead down to evil. Dangers beset them round about, and the pit of destruction yawneth beneath their feet.

Look now on the other side, and behold, in that vale overshadowed with trees, and hid from the sight of men, the habitation of Sorrow.

Her bosom heaveth with sighs, her mouth is filled with lamentation; she delighteth to dwell on the subject of human misery.

She looketh on the common accidents of life, and weepeth; the weakness and wickedness of man is the theme of her lips.

All nature to her teemeth with evil, every object she seeth is tinged with the gloom of her own mind. and the voice of complaint saddeneth her dwelling day and night.

Come not near her cell; her breath is contagious; she will blast the fruits, and wither the flowers that adorn and sweeten the garden of life.

In avoiding the house of joy, let not thy feet betray thee to the borders of this dismal mansion; but pursue with care the middle path, which shall lead thee by a gentle ascent to the bower of Tranquillity.

With her dwelleth Peace, with her dwelleth Safety and Contentment. She is cheerful, but not gay; she is serious, but not grave; she vieweth the joys and the sorrows of life with an equal and steady eye.

From hence, as from an eminence, shalt thou behold the folly and the misery of those who, led by the gaiety of their hearts, take up their abode with the companions of jollity and riotous Mirth; or, infected with gloominess and melancholy, spend all their days in complaining of the woes and calamities of human life.

Thou shalt view them both with pity, and the error of their ways shall keep thy feet from straying.

SECTION III.

ANGER.

As the whirlwind in its fury teareth up trees, and deformeth the face of nature; or as an earthquake in its convulsions overturneth whole cities; so the rage of an angry man throweth mischief around him. Danger and destruction wait on his hand.

But consider, and forget not thine own weakness; so shalt thou pardon the failings of others:

Indulge not thyself in the passion of anger; it is whetting a sword to wound thine own breast, or murder thy friend.

If thou bearest slight provocations with patience, it shall be imputed unto thee for wisdom; and if thou whipest them from thy remembrance, thy heart shall not reproach thee.

Seest thou not that the angry man loseth his understanding? Whilst thou art yet in thy senses, let the wrath of another be a lesson to thyself.

Do nothing in a passion. Why wilt thou put to sea in the violence of a storm?

If it be difficult to rule thine anger, it is wise to prevent it: avoid therefore all occasions of falling into wrath: or guard thyself against them whenever they occur.

A fool is provoked with insolent speeches, but a wise man laugheth them to scorn.

Harbour not revenge in thy breast, it will torment thy heart, and warp its best inclinations.

Be always more ready to forgive than to return an injury: he that watches for an opportunity of revenge, lieth in wait against himself, and draweth down mischief on his own head.

A mild answer to an angry man, like water cast upon the fire, abateth his heat; and from an enemy he shall become thy friend.

Consider how few things are worthy of anger, and thou wilt wonder that any but fools should be wrath.

In folly or weakness it always beginneth;

but remember, and be well assured, it seldom concludeth without repentance.

On the heels of folly treadeth shame; at the back of anger standeth remorse.

SECTION IV.

PITY.

As blossoms and flowers are strewed upon earth by the hand of spring, as the kindness of summer produceth in perfection the bounties of harvest; so the smiles of pity shed blessings on the children of misfortune.

He who pitieth another, recommendeth himself; but he who is without compassion, deserveth it not.

The butcher relenteth not at the bleating of the lamb; neither is the heart of the cruel moved with distress.

But the tears of the compassionate are sweeter than dew-drops falling from roses on the bosom of the spring.

Shut not thine ear therefore against the cries of the poor; neither harden thine heart against the calamities of the innocent.

When the fatherless call upon thee, when the widow's heart is sunk, and she imploreth thy assistance with tears of sorrow; O pity her affliction, and extend thy hand to those who have none to help them.

When thou seest the naked wanderer of the street, shivering with cold, and destitute of habitation; let bounty open thine heart, let the wings of charity shelter him from death, that thine own soul may live.

Whilst the poor man groaneth on the bed of sickness, whilst the unfortunate languish in the horrors of a dungeon, or the hoary head of age lifts up a feeble eye to thee for pity; O how canst thou riot in superfluous enjoyments, regardless of their wants, unfeeling of their woes!

SECTION V.

DESIRE AND LOVE.

Beware, young man, beware of the allurements of wantonness, and let not the harlot tempt thee to her delights.

The madness of desire shall defeat its own pursuits; from the blindness of its rage thou shalt rush upon destruction.

Therefore give not up thy heart to her enticements, neither suffer thy soul to be enslaved by her delusions.

The fountain of health, which must supply the stream of pleasure, shall quickly be dried up, and every spring of joy shall be exhausted.

In the prime of thy life old age shall overtake thee: thy sun shall decline in the morning of thy days.

But when virtue and modesty enlighten her charms, the lustre of a beautiful woman is brighter than the stars of heaven, and the influence of her power it is in vain to resist.

The whiteness of her bosom transcendeth the lily; her smile is more delicious than a garden of roses.

The innocence of her eye is like that of the turtle; simplicity and truth dwell in her heart.

The kisses of her mouth are sweeter than honey; the perfumes of Arabia breathe from her lips.

Shut not thy bosom to the tenderness of love; the purity of its flame shall ennoble thy heart, and soften it to receive the fairest impressions.

PART III.

WOMAN.

PART III.

WOMAN.

Give ear, fair daughter of love, to the instructions of prudence, and let the precepts of truth sink deep in thy heart, so shall the charms of thy mind add lustre to the elegance of thy form: and thy beauty, like the rose it resembleth, shall retain its sweetness when its bloom is withered.

In the spring of thy youth, in the morning of thy days, when the eyes of men gaze on thee with delight, and nature whispereth in thine ear the meaning of their looks; ah! hear with caution their seducing words; guard well thy heart, nor listen to their soft persuasions.

Remember that thou art made man's reasonable companion, not the slave of his passion; the end of thy being is not merely to gratify his loose desire, but to assist him in the toils of life, to soothe him with thy tenderness, and recompense his care with soft endearments.

WOMAN.

Who is she that winneth the heart of man, that subdueth him to love, and reigneth in his breast?

Lo! yonder she walketh in maiden sweetness, with innocence in her mind, and modesty on her cheek.

Her hand seeketh employment, her foot delighteth not in gadding abroad.

She is clothed with neatness, she is fed with temperance; humility and meekness are as a crown of glory circling her head.

On her tongue dwelleth music, the sweetness of honey floweth from her lips.

Decency is in all her words, in her answers are mildness and truth.

Submission and obedience are the lessons of her life, and peace and happiness are her reward.

Before her steps walketh Prudence, and Virtue attendeth at her right hand.

Her eye speaketh softness and love; but discretion with a sceptre sitteth on her brow.

The tongue of the licentious is dumb in her presence, the awe of her virtue keepeth them silent.

When scandal is busy, and the fame of her

neighbour is tossed from tongue to tongue, if charity and good nature open not her mouth, the finger of silence resteth on her lip.

Her breast is the mansion of goodness, and therefore she suspecteth no evil in others.

Happy were the man that should make her his wife; happy the child that should call her mother.

She presideth in the house, and there is peace; she commandeth with judgment, and is obeyed.

She ariseth in the morning, she considers her affairs, and appointeth to every one their proper business.

The care of her family is her whole delight, to that alone she applieth her study: and elegance with frugality is seen in her mansions.

The prudence of her management is an honour to her husband, and he heareth her praise with a secret delight.

She informeth the minds of her children with wisdom: she fashioneth their manners from the examples of her own goodness.

The word of her mouth is the law of their youth, the motion of her eye commandeth their obedience.

She speaketh, and her servants fly; she pointeth, and the thing is done: for the law of love is in their hearts, and her kindness addeth wings to their feet.

In prosperity she is not puffed up; in adversity she healeth the wounds of fortune with patience.

The troubles of her husband are alleviated by her counsels, and sweetened by her endearments: he putteth his heart in her bosom, and receiveth comfort.

Happy is the man that hath made her his wife; happy the child that calleth her mother.

PART IV.

CONSANGUINITY;

OR, NATURAL RELATIONS.

SECTION I.

HUSBAND.

Take unto thyself a wife, and obey the ordinance of God; take unto thyself a wife, and become a faithful member of society.

But examine with care, and fix not suddenly. On thy present choice depends thy future happiness.

If much of her time is destroyed in dress and adornments; if she is enamoured with her own beauty, and delighteth in her own praise; if she laugheth much, and talketh loud; if her foot abideth not in her father's house, and her eyes with boldness rove on the faces of men; though her beauty were as the sun in the firmament of heaven, turn thy face from her charms, turn thy feet from her paths, and suffer not thy soul to be ensnared by the allurements of imagination

But when thou findest sensibility of heart,

joined with softness of manners; an accomplished mind, with a form agreeable to thy fancy; take her home to thy house; she is worthy to be thy friend, thy companion in life, the wife of thy bosom.

O cherish her as a blessing sent thee from heaven. Let the kindness of thy behaviour endear thee to her heart.

She is the mistress of thy house; treat her therefore with respect, that thy servants may obey her.

Oppose not her inclination without cause; she is the partner of thy cares, make her also the companion of thy pleasures.

Reprove her faults with gentleness; exact not her obedience with rigour.

Trust thy secrets in her breast; her counsels are sincere, thou shalt not be deceived.

Be faithful to her bed; for she is the mother of thy children.

When pain and sickness assault her, let thy tenderness soothe her affliction; a look from thee of pity and love shall alleviate her grief, or mitigate her pain, and be of more avail than ten physicians.

Consider the tenderness of her sex, the delicacy of her frame; and be not severe to her weakness, but remember thine own imperfections.

SECTION II.

FATHER.

Consider thou, who art a parent, the importance of thy trust; the being thou hast produced, it is thy duty to support.

Upon thee also it may depend, whether the child of thy bosom shall be a blessing or a curse to thyself; a useful or a worthless member to the community.

Prepare him early with instruction, and season his mind with the maxims of truth.

Watch the bent of his inclination, set him right in his youth, and let no evil habit gain strength with his years.

So shall he rise like a cedar on the mountains; his head shall be seen above the trees of the forest.

A wicked son is a reproach to his father; but he that doth right is an honour to his gray hairs.

The soil is thine own, let it not want cultivation; the seed which thou sowest, that also expect to reap.

Teach him obedience, and he shall bless thee; teach him modesty, and he shall not be ashamed.

Teach him gratitude, and he shall receive benefits; teach him charity, and he shall gain love.

Teach him temperance, and he shall have health; teach him prudence, and fortune shall attend him.

Teach him justice, and he shall be honoured by the world; teach him sincerity, and his own heart shall not reproach him.

Teach him diligence, and his wealth shall increase; teach him benevolence, and his mind shall be exalted.

Teach him science, and his life shall be useful; teach him religion, and his death shall be happy.

SECTION III.

SON.

From the creatures of God let man learn wisdom, and apply to himself the instruction they give.

Go to the desert, my son; observe the young stork of the wilderness; let him speak to thy heart; he beareth on his wings his aged sire, he lodgeth him with safety, and supplieth him with food.

The piety of a child is sweeter than the incense of Persia offered to the sun; yea, more delicious than odours wafted from a field of Arabian spices by the western gales.

Be grateful then to thy father, for he gave thee life; and to thy mother, for she sustained thee.

Hear the words of his mouth, for they are spoken for thy good; give ear to his admonition, for it proceedeth from love.

He hath watched for thy welfare, he hath toiled for thy ease; do honour therefore to his age, and let not his gray hairs be treated with irreverence.

Forget not thy helpless infancy, nor the frowardness of thy youth, and indulge the infirmities of thy aged parents; assist and support them in the decline of life.

So shall their hoary heads go down to the grave in peace; and thine own children, in reverence of thy example, shall repay thy piety with filial love.

SECTION IV.

BROTHERS.

Ye are the children of one father, provided for by his care; and the breast of one mother hath given you suck.

Let the bonds of affection, therefore, unite you, that peace and happiness may dwell in your father's house.

And when ye separate in the world, remember the relation that bindeth you to love and unity; and prefer not a stranger to your own blood.

If thy brother is in adversity, assist him: if thy sister is in trouble, forsake her not.

So shall the fortunes of thy father contribute to the support of his whole race; and his care be continued to you all in your love to each other.

PART V

PROVIDENCE;

OR,

THE ACCIDENTAL DIFFERENCES IN MEN.

SECTION I.

WISE AND IGNORANT.

The gifts of the understanding are the treasures of God; and he appointeth to every one his portion, in what measure seemeth good unto himself.

Hath he endued thee with wisdom? hath he enlightened thy mind with the knowledge of truth? Communicate it to the ignorant, for their instruction; communicate it to the wise, for thine own improvement.

True wisdom is less presuming than folly. The fool is obstinate, and doubteth not; he knoweth all things but his own ignorance.

The pride of emptiness is an abomination; and to talk much is the foolishness of folly. Nevertheless, it is the part of wisdom to bear impertinence with patience, and to pity absurdity.

Yet be not puffed up with thine own conceit, neither boast of superior understanding; the clearest human knowledge is but blindness and folly.

The wise man feeleth his imperfections, and is humbled; he laboureth in vain for his own approbation: but the fool peepeth in the shallow stream of his own mind, and is pleased with the pebbles which he sees at the bottom: he bringeth them up, and showeth them as pearls; and with the applause of his brethren delighteth he himself.

He boasteth attainments in things that are of no worth; but where it is a shame to be ignorant, there he hath no understanding.

Even in the paths of wisdom he toileth after folly; and shame and disappointment are the reward of his labour.

But the wise man cultivates his mind with knowledge: the improvement of arts is his delight, and their utility to the public crowneth him with honour.

Nevertheless the attainment of virtue he accounteth as the highest learning: and the science of happiness is the study of his life.

SECTION II.

RICH AND POOR.

The man to whom God hath given riches, and blessed with a mind to employ them aright, is peculiarly favoured, and highly distinguished.

He looketh on his wealth with pleasure, because it affordeth him the means to do good.

He seeketh out objects of compassion: he enquireth into their wants; he relieveth with judgment, and without ostentation.

He assisteth and rewardeth merit; he encourageth ingenuity, and liberally promoteth every useful design.

He carrieth on great works; his country is enriched, and the labourer is employed; he formeth new schemes, and the arts receive improvement.

He considereth the superfluities of his table as belonging to the poor of his neighbourhood, and he defraudeth them not.

The benevolence of his mind is not checked by his fortune; he rejoiceth therefore in riches, and his joy is blameless.

But woe unto him that heapeth up wealth in abundance, and rejoiceth alone in the possession thereof:

That grindeth the face of the poor, and considereth not the sweat of their brows.

He thriveth on oppression without feeling: the ruin of his brother disturbeth him not.

The tears of the orphan he drinketh as milk; the cries of the widow are music to his ear.

His heart is hardened with the love of wealth; no grief nor distress can make impression upon it.

But the curse of iniquity pursueth him: he liveth in continual fear; the anxiety of his mind, and the rapacious desires of his own soul, take vengeance upon him for the calamities he has brought upon others.

O what are the miseries of poverty, in comparison with the gnawings of this man's heart!

Let the poor man comfort himself, yea, rejoice; for he hath many reasons.

He sitteth down to his morsel in peace; his table is not crowded with flatterers and devourers.

He is not embarrassed with a train of dependants, nor teased with the clamours of solicitation.

Debarred from the dainties of the rich, he escapeth also their diseases.

The bread that he eateth, is it not sweet to his taste? the water he drinketh, is it not pleasant to his thirst? yea, far more delicious than the richest draughts of the luxurious.

His labour preserveth his health, and procureth him a repose to which the downy bed of sloth is a stranger.

He limiteth his desires with humility, and the calm of contentment is sweeter to his soul than all the acquirements of wealth and grandeur.

Let not the rich, therefore, presume on his riches; nor the poor, in his poverty, yield to his despondence; for the providence of God dispenseth happiness to them both.

SECTION III.

MASTERS AND SERVANTS.

Repine not, O man, at the state of servitude: it is the appointment of God, and hath many advantages; it removeth thee from the cares and solicitudes of life.

The honour of a servant is his fidelity; his highest virtues are submission and obedience.

Be patient, therefore, under the reproofs of thy master; and, when he rebuketh thee, answer not again. The silence of thy resignation shall not be forgotten.

Be studious of his interests, be diligent in his affairs, and faithful to the trust which he reposeth in thee.

Thy time and thy labour belong unto him. Defraud him not therefore, for he payeth thee for them.

And thou who art a master, be just to thy servant, if thou expecteth from him fidelity;

and reasonable in thy commands, if thou expectest a ready obedience.

The spirit of a man is in him; severity and rigour may create fear, but can never command his love.

Mix kindness with reproof, and reason with authority: so shall thy admonitions take place in his heart, and his duty shall become his pleasure.

He shall serve thee faithfully from the motive of gratitude; he shall obey thee cheerfully from the principle of love: and fail not thou, in return, to give his diligence and fidelity their proper reward.

SECTION IV.

MAGISTRATES AND SUBJECTS.

O THOU, favourite of heaven, whom the sons of men, thy equals, have agreed to raise to sovereign power, and set as a ruler over themselves; consider the ends and importance of their trust, far more than the dignity and height of thy station.

Thou art clothed in purple, and seated on a throne: the crown of majesty investeth thy temples: the sceptre of power is placed in thy hand: but not for thyself were these ensigns given; not meant for thine own, but the good of thy kingdom.

The glory of a king is the welfare of his people; his power and dominion rest on the hearts of his subjects.

The mind of a great prince is exalted with the grandeur of his situation: he revolveth high things, and searcheth for business worthy of his power.

He calleth together the wise men of his kingdom, he consulteth amongst them with freedom, and heareth the opinions of them all.

He looketh among his people with discernment; he discovereth the abilities of men, and employeth them according to their merits.

His magistrates are just, his ministers are wise, and the favourite of his bosom deceiveth him not.

He smileth on the arts and they flourish; the sciences improve beneath the culture of his hand.

With the learned and ingenious he delighteth himself; he kindleth in their breasts emulation, and the glory of his kingdom is exalted by their labours.

The spirit of the merchant, who extendeth his commerce; the skill of the farmer, who enricheth his lands; the ingenuity of the artist, the improvement of the scholar; all these he honoureth with his favour, or rewardeth with his bounty.

He planteth new colonies, he buildeth strong ships, he openeth rivers for convenience, he formeth harbours for safety; his people abound in riches, and the strength of his kingdom increaseth.

He frameth his statutes with equity and wisdom; his subjects enjoy the fruits of their labour in security; and their happiness consists in the observance of the law.

He foundeth his judgments on the principles of mercy; but in the punishments of offenders he is strict and impartial.

His ears are open to the complaints of his subjects; he restraineth the hand of their oppressors, and delivereth them from their tyranny.

His people therefore look up to him as a father, with reverence and love: they consider him as the guardian of all they enjoy.

Their affection unto him begetteth in his breast a love of the public; the security of their happiness is the object of his care.

No murmurs against him arise in their hearts: the machinations of his enemies endanger not his state.

His subjects are faithful, and firm in his cause; they stand in his defence as a wall of brass; the army of a tyrant flieth before them as chaff before the wind.

Security and peace bless the dwellings of his people; glory and strength encircle his throne for ever.

PART VI.

THE SOCIAL DUTIES.

SECTION I.

BENEVOLENCE.

When thou considerest thy wants, when thou beholdest thy imperfections, acknowledge His goodness, O son of humanity! who honoured thee with reason, endued thee with speech, and placed thee in society, to receive and confer reciprocal helps and mutual obligations.

Thy food, thy clothing, thy convenience of habitation; thy protection from the injuries, thy enjoyments of the comforts and the pleasures of life; all these thou owest to the assistance of others, and couldst not enjoy but in the bands of society.

It is thy duty therefore to be a friend to mankind, as it is thy interest that man should be friendly to thee.

As the rose breatheth sweetness from its own

nature, so the heart of a benevolent man produceth good works.

He enjoyeth the ease and tranquillity of his own breast, and rejoiceth in the happiness and prosperity of his neighbour.

He openeth not his ear unto slander: the faults and the failings of men give a pain to his heart.

His desire is to do good, and he searcheth out the occasions thereof; in removing the oppressions of another he relieveth himself.

From the largeness of his mind, he comprehendeth in his wishes the happiness of all men; and, from the generosity of his heart, he endeavoureth to promote it.

SECTION II.

JUSTICE.

The peace of society dependeth on justice; the happiness of individuals, on the safe enjoyment of all their possessions.

Keep the desires of thy heart, therefore, within the bounds of moderation; let the hand of justice lead them aright.

Cast not an evil eye on the goods of thy neighbour; let whatever is his property be sacred from thy touch.

Let no temptation allure thee, nor any provocation excite thee, to lift up thy hand to the hazard of his life.

Defame him not in his character; bear no false witness against him.

Corrupt not his servant to cheat or forsake him; and the wife of his bosom, O tempt not to sin.

It will be a grief to his heart, which thou

canst not relieve; an injury to his life, which no reparation can atone for.

In thy dealings with men, be impartial and just; and do unto them as thou wouldst they should do unto thee.

Be faithful to thy trust, and deceive not the man who relieth upon thee; be assured it is less evil in the sight of God to steal, than to betray.

Oppress not the poor, and defraud not of his hire the labouring man.

When thou sellest for gain, hear the whisperings of conscience, and be satisfied with moderation; nor from the ignorance of the buyer make any advantage.

Pay the debts which thou owest, for he who gave thee credit, relied upon thine honour; and to withhold from him his due, is both mean and unjust.

Finally, O son of society! examine thy heart, call remembrance to thy aid; and if in any of these things thou findest thou hast transgressed, take sorrow and shame to thyself, and make speedy reparation to the utmost of thy power.

SECTION III.

CHARITY.

Happy is the man who hath sown in his breast the seeds of benevolence; the produce thereof shall be charity and love.

From the fountain of his heart shall rise rivers of goodness; and the streams shall overflow for the benefit of mankind.

He assisteth the poor in their trouble; he rejoiceth in furthering the prosperity of all men.

He censureth not his neighbour, he believeth not the tales of envy and malevolence, neither repeateth he their slanders.

He forgiveth the injuries of men, he wipeth them from his remembrance; revenge and malice have no place in his heart.

For evil he returneth not evil; he hateth not even his enemies, but requiteth their unjustice with friendly admonition.

HE HEALETH THE QUARRELS OF ANGRY MEN.

W. M. Craig del.   Mackenzie sculp.

Published by T. & R. Hughes, Ludgate Street, Jan'. 3, 1809.

The griefs and anxieties of men excite his compassion; he endeavoureth to alleviate the weight of their misfortunes, and the pleasure of success rewardeth his labour.

He calmeth the fury, he healeth the quarrels of angry men, and preventeth the mischiefs of strife and animosity.

He promoteth in his neighbourhood peace and good-will, and his name is repeated with praise and benedictions.

SECTION IX.

GRATITUDE.

As the branches of a tree return their sap to the root from whence it arose; as a river poureth its streams to the sea, where its spring was supplied; so the heart of a grateful man delighteth in returning a benefit received.

He acknowledgeth his obligations with cheerfulness; he looketh on his benefactor with love and esteem.

And if to return it be not in his power, he nourisheth the memory of it in his breast with kindness, he forgetteth it not all the days of his life.

The hand of the generous man is like the clouds of heaven, which drop, upon the earth, fruits, herbage, and flowers: but the heart of the ungrateful is like a desert of sand, which swalloweth, with greediness, the showers that fall, and burieth them in its bosom, and produceth nothing.

Envy not thy benefactor, neither strive to conceal the benefit he hath conferred; for though the act of generosity commandeth admiration; yet the humility of gratitude toucheth the heart, and is amiable in the sight both of God and man.

But receive not a favour from the hands of the proud: to the selfish and avaricious have no obligation: the vanity of pride shall expose thee to shame, the greediness of avarice shall never be satisfied.

SECTION V.

SINCERITY.

O THOU who art enamoured with the beauties of Truth, and hast fixed thy heart on the simplicity of her charms, hold fast thy fidelity unto her and forsake her not; the constancy of thy virtue shall crown thee with honour.

The tongue of the sincere is rooted in his heart: hypocrisy and deceit have no place in his words.

He blusheth at falsehood, and is confounded; but, in speaking the truth, he hath a steady eye.

He supporteth as a man the dignity of his character; to the arts of hypocrisy he scorneth to stoop.

He is consistent with himself; he is never embarrassed; he hath courage enough for truth, but to lie he is afraid.

He is far above the meanness of dissimulation; the words of his mouth are the thoughts of his heart.

Yet with prudence and caution he openeth his lips; he studieth what is right, and speaketh with discretion.

He adviseth with friendship, he reproveth with freedom; and whatsoever he promiseth shall surely be performed.

But the heart of the hypocrite is hid in his breast: he masketh his words in the semblance of truth, while the business of his life is only to deceive.

He laugheth in sorrow, he weepeth in joy; and the words of his mouth have no interpretation.

He worketh in the dark as a mole, and fancieth he is safe; but he blundereth into light, and is betrayed and exposed, with his dirt on his head.

He passeth his days with perpetual constraint; his tongue and his heart are for ever at variance.

He laboureth for the character of a righteous man; and he huggeth himself in the thoughts of his cunning.

O fool, fool! the pains which thou takest to hide what thou art, are more than would make thee what thou wouldst seem; and the children of wisdom shall mock at thy cunning, when, in the midst of security, thy disguise is stripped off, and the finger of derision shall point thee to scorn.

PART VII.

RELIGION.

SECTION I.

RELIGION.

There is but one God, the author, the creator, the governor of the world, almighty, eternal, and incomprehensible.

The sun is not God, though his noblest image. He enliveneth the world with his brightness, his warmth giveth life to the products of the earth; admire him as the creature, the instrument of God; but worship him not.

To the One who is supreme, most wise and beneficent, and to him alone belong worship, adoration, thanksgiving, and praise.

Who hath stretched forth the heavens with his hand, who hath described with his finger the courses of the stars.

Who setteth bounds to the ocean, which it cannot pass; and saith unto the stormy winds, Be still.

Who shaketh the earth, and the nations tremble; who darteth his lightnings, and the wicked are dismayed.

Who calleth forth worlds by the word of his mouth; who smiteth with his arm, and they sink into nothing.

" O reverence the Majesty of the Omnipotent; and tempt not his anger, lest thou be destroyed!"

The providence of God is over all his works; he ruleth, and directeth with infinite wisdom.

He hath instituted laws for the government of the world; he hath wonderfully varied them in all beings; and each, by his nature, conformeth to his will.

In the depth of his mind he revolveth all knowledge; the secrets of futurity lie open before him.

The thoughts of thy heart are naked to his view; he knoweth thy determinations before they are made.

With respect to his prescience, there is nothing contingent; with respect to his providence, there is nothing accidental.

Wonderful he is in all his ways; his counsels are inscrutable; the manner of his knowledge transcendeth thy conception.

"Pay therefore to his wisdom all honour and veneration; and bow down thyself in humble and submissive obedience to his supreme direction."

The Lord is gracious and beneficent; he hath created the world in mercy and love.

His goodness is conspicuous in all his works: he is the fountain of excellence, the centre of perfection.

The creatures of his hand declare his goodness, and all their enjoyments speak his praise; he clotheth them with beauty, he supporteth them with food, he preserveth them with pleasure from generation to generation.

If we lift up our eyes to the heavens, his glory shineth forth; if we cast them down upon the earth, it is full of his goodness; the hills and the vallies rejoice and sing; fields, rivers, and woods resound his praise.

But thee, O man, he hath distinguished with peculiar favour; and exalted thy station above all creatures.

He hath endued thee with reason, to maintain thy dominion; he hath fitted thee with language, to improve by society; and exalted thy mind with the powers of meditation to contemplate and adore his inimitable perfections.

And in the laws he hath ordained, as the rule of thy life, so kindly hath he suited thy duty to thy nature, that obedience to his precepts is happiness to thyself.

"O praise his goodness with songs of thanksgiving, and meditate, in silence, on the wonders of his love; let thy heart overflow with gratitude and acknowledgment; let the language of thy lips speak praise and adoration; let the actions of thy life show thy love to his law."

The Lord is just and righteous, and will judge the earth with equity and truth.

Hath he established his laws in goodness and mercy; and shall he not punish the transgressors thereof?

O think not, bold man! because thy punishment is delayed, that the arm of the Lord is weakened; neither flatter thyself with hopes that he winketh at thy doings.

His eye pierceth the secrets of every heart, and he remembereth them for ever; he respecteth not the persons nor the stations of men.

The high and the low, the rich and the poor, the wise and the ignorant, when the soul hath shaken off the cumbrous shackles of this mortal life, shall equally receive from the sentence of

God a just and everlasting retribution, according to their works.

Then shall the wicked tremble and be afraid; but the heart of the righteous shall rejoice in his judgments.

"O fear the Lord, therefore, all the days of thy life, and walk in the paths which he has opened before thee. Let prudence admonish thee, let temperance restrain, let justice guide thy hand, benevolence warm thy heart, and gratitude to heaven inspire thee with devotion. These shall give thee happiness in thy present state, and bring thee to the mansions of eternal felicity in the paradise of God."

This is the true ECONOMY of HUMAN LIFE.

BOOK SECOND.

PART I.

MAN,
CONSIDERED IN THE GENERAL.

SECTION I.

OF THE HUMAN FRAME AND STRUCTURE.

Weak and ignorant as thou art, O man! humble as thou oughtest to be, O child of the dust! wouldst thou raise thy thoughts to infinite wisdom? wouldst thou see omnipotence displayed before thee? contemplate thine own frame.

Fearfully and wonderfully art thou made: praise therefore thy Creator with awe, and rejoice before him with reverence.

Wherefore of all creatures art thou only erect, but that thou shouldest behold his works! wherefore art thou to behold, but that thou mayest admire them! wherefore to admire, but that thou mayest adore their and thy Creator!

Wherefore is consciousness reposed in thee alone! and whence is it derived to thee.

It is not in flesh to think; it is not in bones to reason. The lion knoweth not that worms shall eat him; the ox perceiveth not that he is fed for slaughter.

Something is added to thee unlike to what thou seest: something informs thy clay, higher than all that is the object of thy senses. Behold, what is it?

Thy body remaineth perfect after this is fled, therefore it is no part of it: it is immaterial, therefore it is eternal: it is free to act, therefore it is accountable for its actions.

Knoweth the ass the use of food, because his teeth mow down the herbage? or standeth the crocodile erect, although his back bone is as straight as thine?

God formed thee as he had formed these: after them all wert thou created; superiority and command were given thee over all, and of his own breath did he communicate to thee thy principle of knowledge.

Know thyself then the pride of his creation; the link uniting divinity and matter: behold a part of God himself within thee: remember thine own dignity, nor dare descend to evil or to meaness.

Who planted terrour in the tail of the serpent? who cloathed the neck of the horse with thunder? even he who hath instructed thee to crush the one under thy feet, and to tame the other to thy purposes.

SECTION II.

OF THE USE OF THE SENSES.

Vaunt not of thy body, because it was first formed; nor of thy brain, because therein thy soul resideth. Is not the master of the house more honourable than its walls?

The ground must be prepared before corn be planted; the potter must build his furnace before he can make his porcelane.

As the breath of Heaven sayeth unto the waters of the deep, this way shall thy billows roll, and no other; thus high shall they raise their fury, and no higher; so let thy spirit, O man, actuate and direct thy flesh; so let it repress its wildness.

Thy soul is the monarch of thy frame; suffer not its subjects to rebel against it.

Thy body is as the globe of the earth, thy bones the pillars that sustain it on its basis.

As the ocean giveth rise to springs, whose waters return again into its bosom through the rivers, so runneth thy life from the heart outwards, and so returneth it unto its place again.

Do not both retain their course for ever? Behold, the same God ordained them.

Is not thy nose the channel to perfumes? thy mouth the path to delicacies? yet know thou, that perfumes long smelt become offensive, that delicacies destroy the appetite they flatter.

Are not thine eyes the sentinels that watch for thee? yet how often are they unable to distinguish truth from error.

Keep then thy soul in moderation, teach thy spirit to be attentive to its good; so shall these its ministers be ever unto thee conveyances of truth.

Thine hand, is it not a miracle? Is there in the creation ought like unto it? wherefore was it given thee, but that thou mightest stretch it out to the assistance of thy brother?

Why of all things living art thou alone made capable of blushing? the world shall read thy shame upon thy face; therefore do nothing shameful.

Fear and dismay, why rob they thy countenance of its ruddy splendour? avoid guilt, and thou shalt know that fear is beneath thee; that dismay is unmanly.

Wherefore to thee alone speak shadows in the visions of thy pillow? reverence them; for know that dreams are from on high.

Thou man alone canst speak. Wonder at thy glorious prerogative; and pay to him who gave it thee a rational and welcome praise, teaching thy children wisdom, instructing the offspring of thy loins in piety.

SECTION III.

THE SOUL OF MAN; ITS ORIGIN AND AFFECTIONS.

The blessings, O man! of thy external part, are health, vigour, and proportion. The greatest of these is health. What health is to the body, even that is honesty to the soul.

That thou hast a soul, is of all knowledge the most certain, of all truth the most plain unto thee. Be meek, be grateful for it. Seek not to know it perfectly. It is inscrutable.

Thought, understanding, reasoning, willing, call not these the soul! they are its actions, but they are not its essence.

Raise it not too high, that thou be not despised. Be not thou like unto those who fall by climbing, neither debase it to the sense of brutes; nor be thou like to the horse and the mule, in whom there is no understanding.

Search it by its faculties, know it by its virtues. They are more in number than the hairs of thy head; the stars of heaven are not to be counted with them.

Think not with Arabia, that one soul is parted among all men; neither believe thou, with the sons of Egypt, that every man hath many: know, that as thy heart, so also thy soul is one.

Doth not the sun harden the clay? doth it not also soften the wax? As it is one sun that worketh both, even so it is one soul that willeth contraries.

As the moon retaineth her nature though darkness spread itself before her face as a curtain, so the soul remaineth perfect even in the bosom of the fool.

She is immortal; she is unchangeable; she is alike in all. Health calleth her forth to shew her loveliness, and application anointeth her with the oil of wisdom.

Although she shall live after thee, think not she was born before thee; she was created with thy flesh, and formed with thy brain.

Justice could not give her to thee exalted by virtues, nor mercy deliver her to thee deformed by vices. These must be thine, and thou must answer them.

Suppose not death can shield thee from examination; think not corruption can hide thee from enquiry. He who formed thee of thou knowest not what, can he not raise thee from thou knowest not what again?

Perceiveth not the cock the hour of midnight? Exalteth he not his voice, to tell thee when it is morning? Knoweth not the dog the footsteps of his master? and flieth not the wounded goat unto the herb that healeth him? Yet, when these die, their spirit returneth to the dust: thine alone surviveth.

Envy not to these their senses, because quicker than thine own. Learn that the advantage lieth not in possessing good things, but in the knowing how to use them.

Hadst thou the ear of the stag, or were thine eye as strong and piercing as the eagle's; didst thou equal the hound in smell; or could the ape resign to thee his taste, or the tortoise her feeling; yet, without reason, what would they avail thee? Perish not all these like their kindred?

Hath any one of them the gift of speech? can any say unto thee, therefore did I so?

The lips of the wise are as the doors of a cabinet? no sooner are they opened, but treasures are poured out before thee.

Like unto trees of gold arranged in beds of silver, are wise sentences uttered in due season.

Canst thou think too greatly of thy soul? or can too much be said in its praise? It is the image of Him who gave it.

Remember thou its dignity for ever; forget not how great a talent is committed to thy charge.

Whatsoever may do good, may also do harm. Beware that thou direct its course to virtue.

Think not that thou canst lose her in the croud; suppose not that canst bury her in thy closet. Action is her delight, and she will not be withheld from it.

Her motion is perpetual; her attempts are universal; her agility is not to be suppressed. Is it at the uttermost part of the earth? she will have it: is it beyond the region of the stars! yet will her eyes discover it.

Inquiry is her delight. As one who traverseth

eth the burning sands in search of water, so is the soul that thirsteth after knowledge.

Guard her, for she is rash; restrain her, for she is irregular; correct her, for she is outragious; more supple is she than water, more flexible than wax, more yielding than air. Is there aught then can bind her?

As a sword in the hand to a madman, even so is the soul to him who wanteth discretion.

The end of her search is truth; her means to discover it are reason and experience, but are not these weak, uncertain, and falacious? How then shall she attain unto it?

General opinion is no proof of truth; for the generality of men are ignorant.

Perception of thyself, the knowledge of Him who created thee, the sense of the worship thou owest unto Him, are not these plain before thy face? And, behold! what is there more that man needeth to know?

SECTION IV.

OF THE PERIOD AND USES OF HUMAN LIFE.

As the eye of morning to the lark, as the shade of evening to the owl, as honey to the bee, or as the carcase to the vulture; even such is life unto the heart of man.

Tho' bright, it dazzleth not; tho' obscure, it displeaseth not; though sweet, it cloyeth not; though corrupt it forbiddeth not; yet who is he that knoweth its true value?

Learn to esteem life as thou oughtest; then art thou near the pinnacle of wisdom.

Think not with the fool, that nothing is more valuable; nor believe with the pretended wise, that thou oughtest to contemn it. Love it not for itself, but for the good it may be of to others.

Gold cannot buy it for thee, neither can the mines of diamonds purchase back the moments thou hast now lost of it. Employ the succeeding ones in virtue.

Say not, that it were best not to have been born; or, if born, that it had been best to die early; neither dare thou to ask of thy Creator, where had been the evil had I not existed; good is in thy power; the want of good is evil; and, if thy question be just, lo! it condemneth thee.

Would the fish swallow the bait if he knew the hook was hid therein? would the lion enter the toils if he saw they were prepared for him? so neither, were the soul to perish with this clay, would man wish to live; neither would a merciful God have created him: know hence thou shalt live afterward.

As the bird inclosed in the cage before he seeth it, yet teareth not his flesh against its sides; so neither labour thou vainly to run from the state thou art in; but know it is allotted thee, and be content with it.

Though its ways are uneven, yet are they not all painful. Accommodate thyself to all; and where there is least appearance of evil, suspect the greatest danger.

When thy bed is straw, thou sleepest in

security; but when thou stretchest thyself on roses, beware of the thorns.

A good death is better than an evil life; strive to live therefore, as long as thou oughest, not as long as thou canst. While thy life is to others worth more than thy death, it is thy duty to preserve it.

Complain not with the fool of the shortness of thy time: remember that with thy days, thy cares are shortened.

Take from the period of thy life the useless parts of it, and what remaineth? Take off the time of thine infancy, the second infancy of age, thy sleep, thy thoughtless hours, thy days of sickness; and, even at the fulness of years, how few seasons hast thou truly numbered.

He who gave thee life as a blessing, shortened it to make it more so. To what end would longer life have served thee; wishest thou to have had an opportunity of more vices? as to the good, will not He who limited thy span, be satisfied with the fruits of it?

To what end, O child of sorrow! wouldst thou live longer? to breathe, to eat, to see the world? all this thou hast done often already.

Too frequent repetition, is it not tiresome? or is it not superfluous.

Wouldst thou improve thy wisdom and virtue? Alas! what art thou to know? or who is it shall teach thee? Badly thou employest the little thou hast, dare not, therefore, to complain that more is not given thee.

Repine not at the want of knowledge; it must perish with thee in the grave. Be honest here, thou shalt be wise hereafter.

Say not unto the crow, why numberest thou seven times the age of thy lord? or to the fawn, why art thine eyes to see my offspring to an hundred generations? are these to be compared with thee in the abuse of life? are they riotous? are they cruel? are they ungreatful? Learn from them rather that innocence of life and simplicity of manners, are the paths to a good old age.

Knowest thou to employ life better than these? then less of it may suffice thee.

Man who dares enslave the world, when he knows he can enjoy his tyranny but a moment, what would he not aim at, if he were immortal?

Enough hast thou of life, but thou regardest not: thou art not in want of it, O man! but thou art prodigal: thou throwest it lightly away, as if thou hast more than enough; and yet thou repinest that it is not gathered again unto thee.

Know that it is not abundance which maketh rich, but economy.

The wise continueth to live from his first period; the fool is always beginning.

Labour not after riches first, and think thou afterwards wilt enjoy them. He who neglecteth the present moment throws away all that he hath. As the arrow passeth through the heart, while the warrior knew not that it was coming; so shall his life be taken away before he knoweth that he hath it.

What then is life, that man should desire it; what is breathing, that he should covet it.

Is it not a scene of delusion, a series of misadventures, a pursuit of evils linked on all sides together; in the beginning it is ignorance, pain is in its middle, and its end is sorrow.

As one wave pusheth on another till both are involved in that behind them, even so succeedeth evil to evil in the life of man; the greater and the present swallow up the lesser and the past. Our terrors are real evils; our expectations look forward into improbabilities.

Fools, to dread as mortals, and to desire as if immortal!

What part of life is it that we would wish to remain with us? Is it youth? can we be in love with outrage, licentiousness, and temerity? Is it age? than are we found of infirmities.

It is said gray hairs are revered, and in length of days is honour. Virtue can add reverence to the bloom of youth; and without it age plants more wrinkles in the soul than on the forehead.

Is age respected because it hateth riot? What justice is in this, when it is not age despiseth pleasure, but pleasure that despiseth age.

Be virtuous while thou art young, so shall thine age be honoured.

PART II.

MAN,

CONSIDERED IN REGARD TO HIS INFIRMITIES AND THEIR EFFECTS.

SECTION I.

VANITY.

Inconstancy is powerful in the heart of man; intemperence swayeth it whither it will; despair engrosseth much of it; and fear proclaimeth, Behold, I set unrival'd therein: but vanity is beyond them all.

Weep not therefore at the calaminities of human state; neither laugh at its follies. In the hands of the man addicted to vanity, life is but the shadow of a dream.

The hero, the most renowned of human characters, what is he but the bubble of this weakness? the public is unstable and ungrateful; why should the man of wisdom endanger himself for fools.

The man who neglecteth his present concerns. to revolve how he will behave when greater, feedeth himself with wind, while his bread is eaten by another.

Act as becometh thee in thy present station; and in more exalted ones thy face shall not be ashamed.

What blindeth the eye, or what hideth the heart of a man from himself, like vanity? Lo! when thou seest not thyself, then others discover thee most plainly.

As the tulip that is gaudy without smell, conspicuous without use; so is the man who setteth himself up on high, and hath not merit.

The heart of the vain is troubled while it seemeth content; his cares are greater than his pleasures.

His solicitude cannot rest with his bones; the grave is not deep enough to hide it; he extendeth his thoughts beyond his being; he bespeaketh praise to be paid when he is gone: but whoso promiseth it, deceiveth him.

As the man who engageth his wife to remain in widowhood, that she disturb not his soul; so is he that expecteth that praise shall reach his ears beneath the earth, or cherish his heart in his shroud.

Do well while thou livest; but regard not what is said of it. Content thyself with deserving praise, and thy posterity shall rejoice in hearing of it.

As the butterfly who seeth not her own colours; as the jessamine which feeleth not the scent it casteth around it; so is the man who appeareth gay, and biddeth others take note of it.

To what purpose, saith he, is my vesture of gold, to what end are my tables filled with dainties, if no eye gaze upon them, if the world know it not! Give thy raiment to the naked, and thy food to the hungry; so shalt thou be praised, and feel that thou deservest it.

Why bestowest thou on every man the flattery of unmeaning words? thou knowest, when returned thee, thou regardest it not. He knoweth he lieth unto thee: yet he knoweth thou wilt thank him for it. Speak in sincerity, and thou shalt hear with instruction.

The vain delighteth to speak of himself; but he seeth not that others like not to hear him.

If he hath done any thing worthy praise; if he possesseth that which is worthy admiration; his joy is to proclaim it: his pride is to hear it reported: the desire of such a man defeateth itself: men say not, behold he hath done it; or, see, he possesseth it; but, mark how proud he is of it.

The heart of man cannot attend at once to many things; he who fixeth his soul on shew, loseth reality: he pursueth bubbles which break in their flight, while he treads to the earth what would do him honour.

SECTION II.

INCONSTANCY.

Nature urgeth thee to inconstancy, O man! therefore guard thyself at all times against it.

Thou art from the womb of thy mother various and wavering; from the loins of thy father inheritest thou instability: how then shalt thou be firm?

Those who gave thee a body, furnished it with weakness; but He who gave thee a soul, armed thee with resolution; employ it, and thou art wise: be wise and thou art happy.

Let him who doeth well, beware how he boasteth of it; for rarely is it of his own will.

Is it not the event of an impulse from without; born of uncertainty; enforced by accident; dependent on somewhat else! to these, then, and to accident, is the praise due.

Beware of irresolution in the intent of thy actions; beware of instability in the execution; so shalt thou triumph over two great failings of thy nature.

What reproacheth reason more than to act contrarieties? what can suppress the tendencies to these, but firmness of mind.

The inconstant feeleth that he changeth, but he knoweth not why; he seeth that he escapeth from himself, but he perceiveth not how; but be thou incapable of change in that which is right; and men will rely upon thee.

Establish unto thyself principles of action; and see that thou ever act according to them.

First know that thy principles are just; and then be thou inflexible in the path of them.

So shall thy passions have no rule over thee: so shall thy constancy ensure unto thee the good thou possessest, and drive from thy door misfortune: anxiety and disapointment shall be strangers to thy gates.

Suspect not evil in any one, until thou seest it: when thou seest it forget it not.

Whoso hath been an enemy cannot be a friend: for a man mendeth not of his faults.

How should his actions be right who hath no rule of life? nothing can be just, which proceedeth not from reason.

The inconstant hath no peace in his soul: neither can any be at ease whom he concerneth himself with.

His life is unequal: his motions are irregular; his soul changeth with the weather.

To-day he loveth thee: to-morrow thou art detested by him: and why? Himself knoweth not wherefore he loved, or wherefore he now hateth.

To-day he is thy tyrant; to-morrow thy servant is less humble; and why? He who is arrogant without power, will be servile where there is no subjection.

To-day he is profuse; to-morrow he grudgeth unto his mouth that which it should eat: thus it is with him that knoweth not moderation.

Who shall say of the cameleon he is black, when the moment after, the verdure of the grass overspreadeth him.

Who shall say of the inconstant, he is joyful, when his next breadth shall be spent in sighing.

What is the life of such a man but the phantom of a dream? in the morning he riseth happy; at noon he is on the rack: this hour he is a god; the next below a worm: one moment he laugheth; the next he weepeth: he now willeth; in an instant he willeth not; and in another he knoweth not whether he willeth or no.

Yet neither ease nor pain have fixed themselves on him; neither is he waxed greater, or become less; neither hath he had cause for laughter, nor reason for sorrow: therefore shall none of them abide with him.

The happiness of the inconstant is as a palace built on the surface of the sand; the blowing of the wind carrieth away its foundation; what wonder then that it falleth.

But what exalted form is this, that hitherward directs its even, its uninterrupted course; whose foot is on the earth, whose head above the clouds?

On his brow sitteth majesty; steadiness is in his port; and in his heart reigneth tranquillity.

Though obstacles appear in his way, he deigneth not to look down upon them; tho' heaven and earth oppose his passage, he proceedeth.

The mountains sink beneath his tread: the

waters of the ocean are dried up under the sole of his foot.

The tiger throweth herself across his way in vain; the spots of the leopard glow against him unregarded.

He marcheth through the embattled legions: with his hand he putteth aside the terrors of death.

Storms roar against his shoulders, but are not able to shake them: the thunder bursteth over his head in vain; the lightning serveth but to shew the glories of his countenance.

His name is Resolution! he cometh from the utmost part of the earth: he seeth happiness afar off before him: his eye discovereth her temple beyond the limits of the pole.

He walketh up to it; he entereth boldly; and he remaineth there for ever.

Establish thy heart, O man! in that which is right, and then know the greatest of human praise is to be immutable.

SECTION III.

WEAKNESS.

Vain and inconstant as thou art, O child of imperfection! how canst thou be but weak? Is not inconstancy connected with frailty? can there be vanity without infirmity? avoid the danger of the one; and thou shalt escape the mischiefs of the other.

Wherein art thou most weak? In that wherein thou seemest most strong: in that wherein most thou gloriest: even in possessing the thing which thou hast; in using the good that is about thee.

Are not thy desires also frail? or knowest thou even what it is thou wouldst wish? when thou hast obtained what most thou soughtest after, behold it contenteth thee not.

Wherefore loseth the pleasure that is before thee its relish? and why appeareth that which is yet to come, the sweeter? because thou art wearied with the good of this, because thou knowest not the evil of that which is not with thee. Know that to be content is to be happy.

Couldst thou chuse for thyself? would thy Creator lay before thee all that thine heart could ask for, would happiness then remain with thee? or would joy dwell always in thy gates?

Alas! thy weakness forbiddeth it! thy infirmity declareth against it. Variety is to thee in the place of pleasure; but that which permanently delighteth must be permanent.

When it is gone thou repentest the loss of it; though while it was with thee, thou despisedst it.

That which succeedeth it, hath no more pleasure for thee; and thou afterwards quarrellest with thyself for preferring it: behold the only circumstance in which thou errest not.

Is their any thing in which thy weakness appeareth more than in desiring things? it is in the possessing, and in the using them.

Good things often cease to be good in our enjoyment of them; what nature meant to be pure sweets, are sources of bitterness to us:

from our delights arise pain: from our joy sorrow.

Be moderate in thy enjoyment; and it shall remain in thy possession: let thy joy be founded on reason; and to its end shall sorrow be a stranger.

The delights of love are ushered in by sighs, and they terminate in languishment and dejection: the object thou burnedst for, nauseates with satiety; and no sooner hadst thou possessed it, but thou wert weary of its presence.

Join esteem to thy admiration; unite friendship with thy love: so shalt thou find in the end, that content surpasseth raptures; that tranquillity is of more worth than extasy.

God has given thee no good without its admixture of evil: but he hath given thee also the means of throwing off the evil from it.

As joy is not without its allay of pain, so neither is sorrow without its portion of pleasure. Joy and grief though unlike are united: our own choice only can give them to us entire.

Melancholy itself often giveth delight: and the extremity of joy is mingled with tears.

The best things in the hand of a fool may

be turned to his destruction: and out of the worst the wise will find the means of good.

So blended is weakness in thy nature, O man! that thou hast not strength either to be good or be evil entirely: rejoice that thou canst not excel in evil: and let the good that is within thy reach content thee.

The virtues are allotted to various stations: seek not after impossibilities, nor grieve that thou canst not possess them all.

Wouldst thou at once have the liberality of the rich, and the contentment of the poor? or should the wife of thy bosom be dispised because she sheweth not the virtues of the widow?

If thy father sink before thee in the divisions of thy country, can at once thy justice destroy him, and thy duty save his life?

If thou behold thy brother in the agonies of a slow death, is it not mercy to put a period to his life? and is it not also death to be his murderer?

Truth is but one; thy doubts are of thine own raising; he who made virtues what they are, planted also in thee a knowledge of their pre-eminence: inform thy soul, and act as that dictates to thee; and the end shall be always right.

SECTION IV.

OF THE
INSUFFICIENCY OF KNOWLEDGE.

If there is any thing lovely; if there is any thing desirable; if there is any thing within the reach of man that is worthy of praise, is it not Knowledge? and yet who is it that attaineth unto it?

The statesman proclaimeth that he hath it: the ruler of the people claimeth the praise of it: but findeth the subject that he possesseth it?

Evil is not requisite to man; neither can vice be necessary to be tolerated; yet how many evils are permitted by the connivance of the laws? how many crimes committed by the decree of the council?

But be wise, O ruler! and learn, O thou that art to command the nations! one crime authorised by thee is worse than the escape of ten from punishment.

When thy people are numerous; when thy sons increase about thy table, sendest thou them not out to slay the innocent; and to fall before the sword of him whom they have not offended?

If the object of thy desire demandeth the lives of a thousand, sayest thou not, I will have it? surely thou forgettest that He who created thee, created also these; and that their blood is as rich as thine.

Sayest thou that justice cannot be executed without wrong? surely thine own words condemn thee.

Thou who flatterest with false hopes the criminal, that he may confess his guilt: art thou not unto him a criminal? or is thy guilt the less because he cannot punish it?

When thou commandest to the torture him who is but suspected of ill; darest thou to remember that thou mayest rack the innocent?

Is thy purpose answered by the event? is thy soul satisfied with his confession? pain will enforce him to say what is not, as easy as what is; and anguish hath caused innocence to accuse herself.

That thou mayest not kill him without cause,

thou dost worse than kill him; that thou mayest prove whether he be guilty, thou destroyest him innocent.

O blindness to all truth! O insufficiency of the wisdom of the wise! know when thy Judge shall bid thee account for this; then shalt thou wish ten thousand guilty to have gone free, rather than one innocent to stand forth against thee.

Insufficient as thou art to the maintenance of Justice, how shalt thou arrive at the knowledge of truth? how shalt thou ascend to the footstep of her throne?

As the owl is blinded by the radiance of the sun, so shall the bright countenance of truth dazzle thee in thy approaches.

If thou wouldest mount up into her throne, first bow thyself at her footstool; if thou wouldest arrive at the knowledge of her, first inform thyself of thine own ignorance.

More worth is she than pearls, therefore seek her carefully; the emerald, and the sapphire, and the ruby, are as dirt beneath her feet; therefore pursue her manfully.

The way to her is labour; attention is the pilot that must conduct thee into her ports:

but weary not in the way; for when thou art arrived at her, the toil shall be to thee for pleasure.

Say not unto thyself, behold truth breedeth hatred, and I will avoid it: dissimulation raiseth friends, and I will follow it: are not the enemies made by truth better than the friends obtained by flattery?

Naturally doth man desire the truth, yet when it is before him, he will not apprehend it; and if it force itself upon him, is he not offended at it?

The fault is not in truth, for that is amiable: but the weakness of man beareth not its splendor.

Wouldst thou see thine insufficiency more plainly; view thyself at thy devotions! To what end was religion instituted, but to teach thee thine infirmities; to remind thee of thy weakness; to shew thee that from heaven alone thou art to hope for good?

Doth it not remind thee that thou art dust? doth it not tell thee that thou art ashes? And behold repentance; is it not built on frailty?

When thou givest an oath; when thou swearest thou wilt not deceive; behold it spreadeth shame upon thy face, and upon the face of him that receiveth it: learn to be just, and repentance may be forgotten; learn to be honest, and oaths are unnecessary.

The shorter follies are the better: say not therefore to thyself, I will not play the fool by halves.

He that heareth his own faults with patience shall reprove another with boldness.

He that giveth a denial with reason, shall suffer a repulse with moderation.

If thou art suspected, answer with freedom: whom should suspicion affright except the guilty?

The tender of heart is turned from his purpose by supplications; the proud is rendered more obstinate by entreaty: the sense of thine insufficiency commandeth thee to hear; but to be just thou must hear without thy passions.

SECTION V.

MISERY.

Feeble and insufficient as thou art, O Man! in good; frail and inconstant as thou art in pleasure! yet is there a thing in which thou art strong and unshaken; its name is Misery.

It is the character of thy being; the prerogative of thy nature: in thy breast alone it resideth; without thee there is nothing of it: and behold what is its source, but thine own passions?

He who gave thee these, gave thee also reason to subdue them; exert it, and thou shalt trample them under thy feet.

Thine entrance into the world, is it not shameful? thy destruction, is it not glorious? Lo! men adorn the instruments of death with gold, and gems, and wear them above their garments.

He who begetteth a man hideth his face; but he that killed a thousand is honoured.

Know thou, notwithstanding, that in this is error: custom can not alter the nature of truth; neither can the opinion of a man destroy justice: the glory and the shame are misplaced.

There is but one way for a man to be produced: there are a thousand by which he may be destroyed.

There is no praise nor honour to him who giveth being to another; but triumphs and empire are the rewards of murder.

Yet he who hath many children, hath as many blessings: and he who hath taken away the life of another, shall not enjoy his own.

While the savage curseth the birth of his son, and blesseth the death of his father; doth he not call himself a monster?

Enough of evil is allotted unto man; but he maketh it more while he lamenteth it.

The greatest of all human ills is sorrow: too much of this thou art born unto; add not unto it by thine own perverseness.

Grief is natural to thee, and is always about thee: Pleasure is a stranger, and visiteth thee but at times: use well thy reason, and sorrow shall be cast behind thee: be prudent, and the visits of Joy shall remain long with thee.

Every part of thy frame is capable of sorrow: but few and narrow are the paths that lead to delight.

Pleasures can be admitted only simply; but pains rush in a thousand at a time.

As the blaze of straw fadeth as soon as it is kindled: so passeth away the brightness of joy, and thou knowest not what is become of it.

Sorrow is frequent; pleasure is rare; pain cometh of itself; delight must be purchased; grief is unmixed; but joy wanteth not its allay of bitterness.

As the soundest health is less perceived than the lightest malady, so the highest joy touches us less deep than the smallest sorrow.

We are in love with anguish; we often fly from pleasure: when we purchase it, costeth it not more than it is worth?

Reflection is the business of man: a sense of his state is his first duty: but who remembereth himself in joy? is it not in mercy then that sorrow is allotted unto us?

Man foreseeth the evil that is to come: he remembereth it when it is past; he considereth not that he thought of affliction woundeth deeper than affliction itself: think not of thy pain but when it is upon thee, and thou shalt avoid what most would hurt thee.

He who weepeth before he needeth, weepeth more than he needeth: and why! but that he loveth weeping.

The stag weepeth not till the spear is lifted up against him: nor do the tears of the beaver fall till the hound is ready to seize him: man anticipateth death by the apprehensions of it: and the fear is greater misery than the event itself.

Be always prepared to give an account of thine actions; and the best death is that which is least premeditated.

SECTION VI.

OF JUDGMENT.

The greatest bounties given to man are, judgment and will: happy is he who misapplieth them not.

As the torrent that rolleth down the mountains, destroyeth all that is borne away by it; so doth common opinion overwhelm reason, in him who submitteth to it, without saying, What is thy foundation?

See that what thou receivest as truth be not the shadow of it; what thou acknowledgest as convincing is often but plausible: be firm, be constant; determine for thyself: so shall thou be answerable only for thine own weakness.

Say not that the event proveth the wisdom of the action: remember man is not above the reach of accidents.

Condemn not the judgments of another, because it differeth from thine own: may not even both be in an error?

When thou esteemest a man for his titles, and contemnest the stranger because he wanteth them, judgest thou not of the camel by his bridle?

Think not thou art revenged of thine enemy when thou slayest him: thou putteth him beyond thy reach; thou givest him quiet; and thou takest from thyself all means of hurting him.

Was thy mother incontinent, and grieveth it thee to be told of it? Is frailty in thy wife, and art thou pained at the reproach of it? he who despiseth thee for it, condemneth himself: art thou answerable for the vices of another?

Disregard not a jewel because thou possessest it: neither enhance thou the value of a thing because it is another's: possession to the wise addeth to the price of it.

Honour not thy wife the less because she is in thy power: and despise him that hath said, Wouldst thou love her less? marry her! What hath put her into thy power, but her confidence in thy virtue? shouldst thou love her less for being more obliged to her?

If thou wert just in thy courtship of her, though thou neglectest her while thou hast her, yet shall her loss be bitter to thy soul.

He who thinketh another best only because he possesseth her; if he be not wiser than thee at least he is more happy.

Weigh not the loss thy friend hath suffered, by the tears he sheddeth, the greatest griefs are oft above the expressions of them.

Esteem not an action because it is done with noise and pomp: the noblest soul is that which doth great things, and is not moved in the doing them.

Fame astonisheth the ear of him who heareth it; but tranquillity rejoiceth the heart that is possessed of it.

Attribute not the good actions of another to bad causes; thou canst not know his heart: but the world will know by this that thine is full of envy.

There is not in hypocrisy more vice than folly: to be honest is as easy as to seem so.

Be more ready to acknowledge a benefit than to revenge an injury; so shalt thou have more benefits than injuries done unto thee.

Be more ready to love than to hate; so shalt thou be loved by more than hate thee.

Be willing to commend, and be slow to censure: so shall praise be upon thy virtues, and the eye of Enmity shall be blind to thy imperfections.

When thou dost good, do it because it is good; not because men esteem it: when thou avoidest evil, flee it because it is evil; not because men speak against it: be honest for love of honesty and thou shalt be uniformly so: he that doth it without principle, is wavering.

Wish rather to be reproved by the wise than to be applauded by him who hath no understanding: when they tell thee of a fault, they suppose thou canst improve; the other, when he praiseth thee, thinketh thee like unto himself.

Accept not an office for which thou art not qualified, lest he who knoweth more of it, despise thee.

Instruct not another in that wherein thyself art ignorant: when he seeth it he will upbraid thee.

Expect not a friendship with him who hath injured thee: he who suffereth the wrong, may forgive; but he who doeth it, it never will be well with him.

Lay not too great obligations on him thou wishest thy friend; behold! the sense of them will drive him from thee: a little benefit alienateth friendship; a great one maketh an enemy.

Nevertheless, ingratitude is not in the nature of man; neither is his anger irreconcileable: he hateth to be put in mind of a debt he cannot pay; he is ashamed in the presence of him whom he hath injured.

Repine not at the good of a stranger; neither rejoice thou in the evil that befalleth thine enemy: Wishest thou that others should do thus by thee?

Wouldst thou enjoy the good-will of all men, let thy own benevolence be universal. If thou obtainest it not by this, no other means could give it thee: and know, though thou hast it not, thou hast the greater pleasure of having merited it.

SECTION VII.

PRESUMPTION.

Pride and meanness seem incompatible; but man reconcileth contrarities: he is at once the most miserable and the most arrogant of all creatures.

Presumption is the bane of reasoning; it is the nurse of error; yet it is congenial with reason in us.

Who is there that judgeth not either too highly of himself, or thinketh too meanly of others.

Our Creator himself escapeth not our presumption: how then shall we be safe from one another?

What is the origin of superstition? And whence ariseth false worship? From our presuming to reason about what is above our reach: to comprehend what is incomprehensible.

Limited and weak as our understandings are, we employ not even their little forces as we ought: we soar not high enough in our approaches to God's greatness; we give not wing enough to our ideas, when we enter into the adoration of Divinity.

Man who fears to breathe a whisper against his earthly sovereign, trembles not to arraign the dispensations of his God; he forgetteth his majesty, and rejudgeth his judgments.

He who dareth not repeat the name of his prince without honour; yet blusheth not to call that of his Creator to be witness to a lie.

He who would hear the sentence of the magistrate with silence; yet dareth to plead with the Eternal: he attempteth to sooth him with intreaties; to flatter him with promises; to agree with him upon conditions; nay, to brave and murmur at him if his request is not granted.

Why art thou unpunished, O man, in thy impiety! but that this is not the day of retribution.

Be not like unto those who fight with the thunder, nor dare thou to deny thy Creator thy prayers because he chastiseth thee: thy madness is on thine own head in this; thy impiety hurteth no one but thyself.

Why boasteth man that he is the favourite of his Maker; yet neglecteth to pay his thanks, his adorations for it? how suiteth such a life with a belief so haughty?

Man, who is truly but a mote in the wide expanse, believeth the whole earth and heaven created for him: he thinketh the whole frame of nature hath interest in his well-being.

As the fool, while the images tremble on the bosom of the water, thinketh that trees, towns, and the wide horizon are dancing to do him pleasure; so man, while nature is performing her destined course, believes that all her emotions are but to entertain his eye.

While he courts the rays of the sun to warm him, he supposeth it made only to be of use to him: while he traceth the moon in her nightly path, he believeth she was created to do him pleasure.

Fool to thine own pride! be humble! know thou art not the cause why the world holdeth its course; for thee are not made the vicissitudes of summer and winter.

No change would follow if thy whole race

existed not: thou art but one among millions that are blessed in it.

Exalt not thyself to the heavens; for, lo, the angels are above thee; nor disdain thy fellow-inhabitants of the earth, for that they are beneath thee; are they not the work of the same hand?

Thou who art happy by the mercy of thy Creator, how darest thou in wantonness put others of his creatures to torture? beware that it return not upon thee.

Serve they not all the same universal Master with thee? hath he not appointed unto each its laws? hath he not care of their preservation? and darest thou infringe it?

Set not thy judgment above that of all the earth? neither condemn as falsehood what agreeth not with thine own apprehension. Who gave thee the power of determining for others; or who took from the world the right of choice.

How many things have been rejected which now are received as truths? how many now received as truths shall in their turn be despised? of what then can man be certain?

Do the good that thou knowest, and happiness shall be unto thee; virtue is more thy business here than wisdom.

Truth and falsehood, have they not the same appearance in what we understand not? what then but our presumption can determine between them?

We easily believe what is above our comprehension; or we are proud to pretend it, that we may appear to have understanding: Is not this folly and arrogance?

Who is it that affirms most boldly? who is it that holds his opinion most obstinately? even he who hath most ignorance; for he also hath most pride.

Every man when he layeth hold of an opinion desireth to remain in it; but most of all he who hath most presumption; he contenteth not himself to betray his own soul into it, but he will impose it on others to believe in it also.

Say not that truth is established by years, or that in a multitude of believers there is certainty.

One human proposition hath as much authority as another, if reason maketh not the difference.

PART III.

OF THE AFFECTIONS OF MAN
WHICH ARE HURTFUL TO HIMSELF AND OTHERS.

SECTION. I.

COVETOUSNESS.

Riches are not worthy a strong attention: an earnest care of obtaining them is therefore unjustifiable.

The desire of what man calleth good, the joy he taketh in possessing it, is grounded only in opinion: take not up that from the vulgar; examine the worth of things thyself, and thou shalt not be covetous.

An immoderate desire of riches is a poison lodged in the soul; it contaminates and destroys every thing that was good in it; it is no sooner rooted there, than all virtue, all honesty, all natural affection, fly before the face of it.

The covetous would sell his children for gold: his parents might die ere he would open his coffer: nay, he considereth not himself in respect of it: in the search of happiness he maketh himself unhappy.

As the man who selleth his house to purchase ornaments for the embellishment of it? even so is he who giveth up peace in the search of riches, in hopes he may be happy in enjoying them.

Where covetousness reigneth, know that the soul is poor. Whoso accounteth not riches the principal good man, will not throw away all other goods in the pursuit of them.

Whoso feareth not poverty as the greatest evil of his nature, will not purchase to himself all other evils in the avoiding of it.

Thou fool, is not virtue more worth than riches? Is not guilt more base than poverty? Enough for his necessities is in the power of every man: be content with it, and thy happiness shall smile at the sorrows of him who heapeth up more.

Nature hath hid gold beneath the earth, as unworthy to be seen; silver hath she placed where thou tramplest it under thy feet: meaneth she not by this to inform thee, that gold is nor worthy thy regard? that silver is beneath thy notice?

Covetousness burieth under the ground millions of wretches: they dig for their hard masters what returneth the injury; what maketh them more miserable than these their slaves.

The earth is barren of good things where she hoardeth up treasure: where gold is in her bowels, there no herb groweth.

As the horse findeth not there is grass, nor the mule his provender; as the fields of corn laugh not on the sides of the hills; as the olive holdeth not forth there her fruits, nor the vine her clusters; even so no good dwelleth in the breast of him whose heart broodeth over his treasure.

Riches are servants to the wise; but they are tyrants over the soul of the fool.

The covetous serveth his gold, it serveth not him: he possesseth his wealth as the sick doth a fever; it burneth and tortureth him, and will not quit him until death.

Hath not gold destroyed the virtue of millions? Did it ever add to the goodness of any?

Is it not most abundant with the worst of men? wherefore then shouldest thou desire to be distinguished by possessing it?

Have not the wisest been those who have had least of it? and is not wisdom happiness?

Have not the worst of thy species possessed the greatest portions of it? and hath not their end been miserable?

Poverty wanteth many things? but covetousness denieth itself all.

The covetous can be good to no man; but he is to none so cruel as to himself.

Be industrious to procure gold: and be generous in the disposal of it; man never is so happy as when he giveth happiness to another.

SECTION II.

PROFUSION.

If there be a vice greater than the hoarding up of riches, it is the employing them to useless purposes.

He that prodigally lavisheth that which he hath to spare, robbeth the poor of what nature giveth them a right unto.

He who squandereth away his treasure refuseth the means to do good: he denieth himself the practice of virtues whose reward is in their hand: whose end is no other than his own happiness.

It is more difficult to be well with riches, than to be at ease under the want of them: man governeth himself much easier in poverty than in abundance.

Poverty requireth but one virtue, patience to support it: the rich, if he hath not charity, temperance, prudence, and many more, is guilty.

The poor hath only the good of his own state committed unto him; the rich is entrusted with the welfare of thousands.

He that giveth his treasures wisely, giveth away his plagues: he that retaineth their increase, heapeth up sorrows.

Refuse not unto the stranger that which he wanteth; deny not unto thy brother even that which thou wantest thyself.

Know there is more delight in being without what thou hast given, than in possessing millions which thou knowest not the use of.

SECTION III.

REVENGE.

The root of revenge is in the weakness of the soul: the most abject and timorous are the most addicted to it.

Who torture those they hate, but cowards? who murder those they rob, but women?

The feeling an injury must be previous to the revenging it; but the noble mind disdaineth to say it hurts me.

If the injury is not below thy notice, he that doeth it unto thee, maketh himself so: wouldst thou enter the lists with thine inferior?

Disdain the man who attempteth to wrong thee; contemn him who would give thee disquiet.

In this thou not only preserveth thine own peace, but thou inflictest all the punishment of revenge, without stooping to employ it against him.

As the tempest and thunder affect not the sun or the stars, but spend their fury on stones and trees below; so injuries ascend not to the souls of the great, but waste themselves on such as are those who offer them.

Poorness of spirit will actuate revenge; greatness of soul despiseth the offence; nay, it doth good unto him who intended to have disturbed it.

Why seekest thou vengeance, O man! with what purpose is it that thou pursuest it? thinkest thou to pain thine adversary by it? know that thyself feelest its greatest torment.

Revenge gnaweth the heart of him who is infected with it; while he against whom it is intended remaineth easy.

It is unjust in the anguish it inflicts; therefore nature intended it not for thee: needeth he who is injured, more pain? or ought he to add force to the affliction which another hath cast upon him?

The man who meditateth revenge is not content with the mischief he hath received. He addeth to his anguish the punishment due unto another; while he whom he seeketh to hurt, goeth away laughing: he maketh himself merry at this addition to his misery.

Revenge is painful in the intent; and it is dangerous in the execution: seldom doth the ax fall where he who lifted it up intended; and lo! he remembereth not that it must recoil against him.

Whilst the revengeful seeketh his enemy's hurt, he often procureth his own destruction: while he aimeth at one of the eyes of his adversary, lo! he putteth out both his own.

If he attain not his end, he lamenteth it: if he succeed, he repenteth of it. The fear of justice taketh away the peace of his own soul; the care to hide him from it, destroyeth that of his friend.

Can the death of thine adversary satiate thy hatred? can the setting him at rest restore thy peace?

Wouldst thou make him sorry for his offence, conquer him and spare him: in death he owneth not thy superiority: nor feeleth he more the power of thy wrath.

In revenge their should be a triumph of the avenger; and he who hath injured him should feel his displeasure; he should suffer pain from it, and should repent him of the cause.

This is the revenge inspired from anger; but that which maketh the greatest, is contempt.

Murder for an injury ariseth only from cowardice: he who inflicted it feareth that the enemy may live and avenge himself.

Death ended the quarrel; but it restoreth not the reputation: killing is an act of caution, not of courage; it is safe, but it is not honourable.

There is nothing so easy as to revenge an offence; but nothing is so honourable as to pardon it.

The greatest victory man can obtain is over himself: he that disdaineth to feel an injury retorteth it upon him who offereth it.

When thou meditatest revenge, thou confessest that thou feelest the wrong; when thou complainest, thou acknowledgest thyself hurt by it; meanest thou to add this triumph to the pride of thine enemy?

That cannot be an injury which is not felt: how then can he who despiseth it, revenge it.

If thou think it dishonourable to bear an offence, more is in thy power; thou mayest conquer it.

Good offices will make a man ashamed to be thine enemy. Greatness of soul will terrify him from the thought of hurting thee.

The greater the wrong, the more glory is in pardoning it; and by how much more justifiable would be revenge, by so much the more honour is in clemency.

Hast thou a right to be a judge in thine own cause; to be a party in the act, and yet to pronounce sentence on it? before thou condemnest, let another say it is just.

The revengeful is feared, and therefore he is hated: but he that is endowed with clemency is adored. The praise of his actions remaineth for ever; and the love of the world attendeth him.

SECTION IV.

CRUELTY, HATRED, AND ENVY,

Revenge is detestable: what then is cruelty? lo! it possesseth the mischiefs of the other, but it wanteth even the pretence of its provocations.

Men disown it as not of their nature: they are ashamed of it as a stranger to their hearts: do they not call it inhumanity?

Whence then is her origin? unto what that is human oweth she her existence? her father is Fear; and behold Dismay, is it not her mother.

The hero lifted his sword against the enemy that resisteth; but no sooner doth he submit, than he is satisfied.

It is not in honour to trample on the object that feareth: it is not in virtue to insult what is beneath it: subdue the insolent, and spare the humble, and thou art at the height of victory.

CRUELTY HATRED & ENVY.

He who wanteth virtue to arrive at this end; he who hath not courage to ascend thus into it: lo! he supplieth the place of conquest by murder, of sovereignty by slaughter.

He who feareth all, striketh at all: why are tyrants cruel, but because they live in terror?

The cur will tear the carcase, though he dare not look it in the face while living: but the hound who hunteth it to the death, mangleth it not afterwards.

Civil wars are the most bloody, because those who fight them are cowards. Conspirators are murderers, because in death there is silence: is it not Fear that telleth them they may be betrayed?

That thou mayest not be cruel, set thyself too high for hatred.

That thou mayest not be inhuman, place thyself above the reach of envy.

Every man may be viewed in two lights: in one he will be troublesome, in the other less offensive: choose to see him in that in which he least hurteth thee; then shalt thou do no hurt unto him.

What is there that a man may not turn unto his good? in that which offendeth us most, there is more ground for complaint than hatred. Man would be reconciled to him of whom he complaineth: what murdereth he, but what he hateth?

If thou art prevented of a benefit, fly not into rage: the loss of thy reason is the want of a greater.

Because thou art robbed of thy cloak, wouldst thou strip thyself of thy coat also?

When thou enviest the man who possesseth honours; when his titles and his greatness raise thy indignation; seek to know whence they came unto him; enquire by what means he was possessed of them, and thine envy will be turned into pity.

If the same fortune were offered unto thee at the same price, be assured if thou wert wise thou wouldst refuse it.

What is the pay for titles but flattery? how doth man purchase power but by being a slave to him who giveth it?

Wouldst thou lose thine own liberty to be able to take away that of another! or canst thou envy him who doth so?

Man purchaseth nothing of his superiors but

for a price, and that price, is it not more than the value? wouldst thou prevert the customs of the world? wouldst thou have the purchase and the price also?

As thou canst not envy what thou wouldst not accept, disdain this cause of hatred; and drive from thy soul this occasion as the parent of cruelty.

If thou possessest honour, canst thou envy that which is obtained at the expence of it? if thou knowest the value of virtue, pitiest thou not those who have bartered it so meanly?

When thou hast taught thyself to bear the seeming good of men without repining, thou wilt hear of their real happiness with pleasure.

If thou seest good things fall to one who deserveth them, thou wilt rejoice in it; for virtue is happy in the prosperity of the virtuous.

He who rejoiceth in the happiness of another, increaseth by it his own.

SECTION V.

HEAVINESS OF HEART.

The soul of the chearful forceth a smile from the face of affliction; but the despondence of the sad, deadeneth even the brightness of Joy.

What is the source of sadness, but a feebleness of the soul? what giveth it power, but the want of spirit? rouse thyself to the combat, and she quitteth the field before thou strickest.

She is an enemy to thy race; therefore drive her from thy heart; she poisoneth the sweets of thy life; therefore suffer her not to enter thy dwelling.

She raiseth the loss of a straw to the destruction of thy fortune; while she vexeth thy soul about trifles, she robbeth thee of thine attention to the things of consequence; behold, she but prophesieth what she seemeth to relate unto thee.

She spreadeth drowsiness as a veil over thy virtues: she hideth them from those who would honour thee on beholding them: she entangleth and keepeth them down, while she maketh it most necessary for thee to exert them.

Lo! she oppresseth thee with evil; and she tieth down thine hands, when they would throw the load from off thee.

If thou wouldst avoid what is base; if thou wouldst disdain what is cowardly; if thou wouldst drive from thy heart what is unjust, suffer not sadness to lay hold upon it.

Suffer it not to cover itself with the face of piety; let it not deceive thee with a show of wisdom. Religion payeth honour to thy Maker; let it not be clouded with melancholy: wisdom maketh thee happy: know then that sorrow in her sight is as a stranger.

For what should man be sorrowful, but for afflictions? why should his heart give up joy, when the causes of it are not removed from him? is not this being miserable for the sake of misery?

As the mourner who looketh sad because he

is hired to do so; who weepeth because his tears are paid for: such is the man who suffereth his heart to be sad, not because he aileth ought, but because he is gloomy.

It is not the occasion that produceth the sorrow; for behold the same thing shall be to another rejoicing.

Ask men if their sadness maketh things the better, and themselves confess to thee that it is folly; nay they will praise him who beareth his ills with patience, who maketh head against misfortunes with courage, applause should be followed by imitation.

Sadness is against nature, for it troubleth her motions; lo! it rendereth distasteful whatever she hath made amiable.

As the oak falleth before the tempest and raiseth not his head again: so boweth the heart of man to the force of sadness, and returneth unto its strength no more.

As the snow melteth upon the mountains from the rain that trickleth down their sides, even so is beauty washed from off the cheeks by tears: and 'neither the one nor the other returneth again for ever.

As the pearl is dissolved by the vinegar which

seemeth at first only to obscure its surface; so is thy happiness, O man, swallowed up by heaviness of heart, though at first it seemeth only to cover it with its shadow.

Behold sadness in the public streets: cast thine eye upon her in the places of resort: doth any look upon her? avoideth she not every one? and doth not every one flee from her presence?

See how she droopeth her head like a flower whose root is cut asunder: see how she fixeth her eyes on the earth, see how they serve her to no purpose but for weeping.

Is there in her mouth discourse? is there in her heart the love of society? is there in her soul reason? ask her the cause, and she knoweth it not: inquire the occasion, and behold there is none.

Yet doth her strength fail her; lo! at length she sinketh into the grave, and no one sayeth, what is become of her?

Hast thou understanding and seest thou not this? hast thou piety, and perceivest thou not thine error?

God created thee in mercy: had he not intended thee to be happy his beneficence would not have called thee into existence; how darest thou then to fly in the face of his majesty?

While thou art most happy with innocence, thou dost him most honour; and what is thy discontent, but murmuring against him?

Created he not all things liable to changes? and darest thou to weep at their changing?

If we know the law of nature, wherefore do we complain of it? if we are ignorant of it, what should we accuse but our blindness, to what every moment giveth us proof of?

Know, that it is not thou that art to give laws to the world: thy part is to submit to them as thou findest them: if they distress thee, thy lamenting is but adding to thy torment.

Be not deceived with fair pretences, nor suppose that sorrow healeth misfortune: it is a poison under the colour of remedy; while it pretendeth to draw the arrow from thy breast, lo! it plungeth it into thine heart.

While sadness separateth thee from thy friends, doth it not say thou art unfit for conversation? while it driveth thee into corners, doth it not proclaim that it is ashamed of itself?

It is not in thy nature to meet the arrows of ill fortune unhurt; nor doth reason require it of thee: it is thy duty to bear misfortune like a man; but thou must first also feel it like one.

Tears may drop from thine eyes: be thou careful only that there is cause; and that they flow not too abundantly.

The greatness of the evil is not to be reckoned from the number of tears shed for it; the greatest griefs are above these testimonies, as the greatest joys are beyond utterance.

What is there that weakeneth the soul like grief? what depresseth it like sadness?

Is the sorrowful prepared for noble enterprises? or armeth he himself in the cause of virtue?

Subject not thyself to ills, where there are in return no advantages; neither sacrifice thou the means of good unto that which is in itself an evil.

PART IV.

OF THE
ADVANTAGES MAN MAY ACQUIRE
OVER HIS FELLOW-CREATURES.

SECTION I.

NOBILITY AND HONOUR.

Nobility resideth not but in the soul; nor is there true honour except in virtue.

The favour of princes may be bought by vices; rank and titles may be purchased for money: but these are not true honour.

Crimes cannot exalt the man who commits them to real glory; neither can gold make men noble.

When titles are the reward of virtue; when he is set on high who hath served his country: he who bestoweth the honours hath glory, like as he who receiveth them; and the world is benefited by it.

Wouldst thou wish to be raised and men know not for what; wouldst thou that they should say, why is this?

When the virtues of the hero descend to his

children, his titles accompany them well: but when he who possesseth them is unlike to him who deserveth them, lo! do they not call him degenerate?

Hereditary honour is accounted the most noble; but reason speaketh in the cause of him who hath acquired it.

He who, meritless himself, appealeth to the actions of his ancestors for his greatness, is like a thief who claimeth protection by flying to the Pagod.

What good is it to the blind, that his parents could see? what benefit is it to the dumb, that his grandfather was eloquent? even so what is it to the mean, that their predecessors were noble?

A mind disposed to virtue, maketh great the possessor of it: and without titles it will raise him above the vulgar.

He will acquire honour while others receive it: and will he not say unto them, such were the men whom you glory in being derived from.

As the shadow waiteth upon the substance, even so true honour attendeth upon virtue.

Say not that honour is the child of boldness, nor believe thou that the hazard of life alone can pay the price of it: it is not to the action that it is due, but to the manner of performing it.

All are not called to the guiding the helm of state; neither are there armies to be commanded by every one: do well in that which is committed to thy charge, and praise shall remain upon thee.

Say not that difficulties are necessary to be conquered, or that labour and danger must be in the way to renown; the woman who is chaste, is she not praised? the man who is honest, deserveth he not to be honoured?

The thirst of fame is violent; the desire of honour is powerful; and he who gave them to us, gave them for great purposes.

When desperate actions are necessary to the public; when our lives are to be exposed for the good of our country, what can add force to virtue but ambition?

It is not the receiving honour that delighteth the noble mind; its pride is the deserving it.

Is it not better men should say, why hath not this man a statue! than that they should ask, why he hath one?

The ambitious will always be first in the crowd; he presseth forward, he looketh out behind him; more anguish is it to his soul to see one before him, than joy to leave thousands at a distance.

The root of ambition is in every man; but it riseth not in all: fear keepeth it down in some, in many it is suppressed by modesty.

It is the inner garment of the soul; the first thing put on by it with the flesh, and the last it layeth down at its separation from it.

It is an honour to thy nature when worthily employed; when thou directest it to wrong purposes, it shameth and destroyeth thee.

In the breast of the traitor ambition is covered: Hypocrisy hideth her face under her mantle, and cool dissimulation furnisheth it with smooth words: but in the end men shall see what it is.

The serpent loseth not his sting though benumbed with the frost; the tooth of the viper is not broken, though the cold closeth his mouth: take pity on his state and he will shew thee his spirit: warm him in thy bosom and he will requite thee with death.

He that is truly virtuous, loveth Virtue, for herself: he disdaineth the applause which ambition aimeth after.

How pitiable were the state of Virtue, if she could not be happy but from another's praise! she is too noble to see recompence, and no more will, than can be rewarded.

The higher the sun ariseth, the less shadow doth it make; even so the greater is the virtue, the less doth it covet praise; yet cannot it avoid its reward in honours.

Glory, like a shadow, flieth him who pursueth it; but it followeth at the heels of him who would fly from it: if thou courtest it without merit, thou shalt never attain unto it; if thou deservest it, though thou hidest thyself, it will never forsake thee

Pursue that which is honourable, do that which is right, and the applause of thine own conscience will be more joy to thee, than the shouts of millions who know not that thou deservest them.

SECTION II.

SCIENCE AND LEARNING.

The noble employment of the mind of man is the study of the works of his Creator.

To him whom the science of nature delighteth, every object bringeth a proof of his God; every thing that proveth it, giveth cause of adoration:

His mind is lifted up to heaven every moment; his life is one continued act of devotion.

Casteth he his eye towards the clouds, findeth he not the heavens full of wonders? looketh he down to the earth, doth not the worm proclaim to him,—Could less than Omnipotence have formed me?

While the planets perform their courses; while the sun remaineth in his place; while the comet wandereth through the liquid air, and returneth to its destined road again; who but thy God, O man! could have formed them? what but infinite Wisdom could have appointed them their laws?

Behold how awful their splendour? yet do they not diminish! lo! how rapid their motions! yet one runneth not in the way of another.

Look down upon the earth, and see her produce: examine her bowels, and behold what they contain; hath not wisdom and power ordained the whole?

Who biddeth the grass to spring up? who watereth it at its due seasons? behold the ox croppeth it; the horse and the sheep, feed not they upon it? who is he that provideth it for them?

Who giveth increase to the corn which thou sowest? who returneth it to thee a thousand fold?

Who ripeneth for thee the olive in its time? and the grape also, though thou knowest not the cause of it.

Can the meanest fly create itself? or wert

thou any less than God, couldst thou have fashioned it?

The beasts feel that they exist; but they wonder not at it: they rejoice in their life, but they know not that it shall end: each performeth its course in succession: nor is there a loss of one species in a thousand generations.

Thou who seest the whole as admirable as its parts, canst thou better employ thine eye than in tracing out thy Creator's greatness in them; thy mind, than in examining their wonders?

Power and mercy are displayed in their formation; justice and goodness shine forth in the provision that is made for them: all are happy in their several ways, nor envieth one the other.

What is the study of words compared with this? in what science is knowledge, but in the study of Nature.

When thou hast adored the fabric, enquire into its use; for know, the earth produceth nothing but may be of good to thee: are not food and raiment, and the remedies for thy diseases, all derived from this source alone?

Who is wise then, but he that knoweth it? who hath understanding, but he that contemplateth it? for ther est, whatever science hath most utility;

whatever knowledge hath the least vanity; prefer these unto the others; and profit of them for the sake of thy neighbour.

To live and to die; to command and to obey; to do and to suffer; are not these all that thou hast further to care about? morality shall teach thee these: the Economy of Life shall lay them before thee.

Behold they are written in thine heart, and thou needest only to be reminded of them; they are easy of conception; be attentive, and thou shalt retain them.

All other sciences are vain, all other knowledge is boast, lo! it is not necessary or beneficial to Man, or doth it make him more good or more honest.

Piety to thy God, and benevolence to thy fellow-creatures, are they not thy great duties? what shall teach thee the one like the study or his works? what shall inform thee of the other like understanding thy dependencies.

PART V.

OF NATURAL ACCIDENTS.

SECTION I.

PROSPERITY AND ADVERSITY.

Let not prosperity elate thine heart above measure; neither depress thy soul to the grave, because Fortune beareth hard against thee.

Her smiles are not stable; therefore build not thy confidence upon them: her frowns endure not for ever; therefore let hope teach thee patience.

To bear adversity well is difficult: but to be temperate in prosperity is the height of wisdom.

Good and ill are the tests by which thou art to know thy constancy; nor is there aught else that can tell thee the powers of thine own soul; be therefore upon the watch when they are upon thee.

Behold prosperity, how sweetly she flattereth thee; how insensibly she robbeth thee of thy strength and thy vigour!

Though thou hast been constant in ill fortune; though thou hast been invincible in distress; yet by her thou art conquered; not knowing that thy strength returneth not again, and yet that thou again mayest need it.

Affliction moveth our enemies to pity; success and happiness causeth even our friends to envy.

Adversity is the seed of well-doing! it is the nurse of all heroism and boldness: who that hath enough will endanger himself to have more? who that is at ease will set his life on the hazard?

True virtue will act under all circumstances; but men see most of its effects when accidents concur with it.

In adversity man seeth himself abandoned by others; he findeth that all his hopes are centered within himself: he rouseth his soul, he encountereth his difficulties, and they yield before him.

In prosperity he fancieth himself safe; he thinketh he is beloved of all that smile about his table: he groweth careless and remiss: he seeth not the danger that is before him: he trusteth to others, and in the end they deceive him.

Every man can advise his own soul in distress; but prosperity blindeth the truth.

Better is the sorrow that leadeth to contentment, than the joy that rendereth man unable to endure distress; and afterwards plungeth him into it.

Our passions dictate to us in all our extremes: moderation is the effect of wisdom.

Be upright in thy whole life; be content in all its changes; so shalt thou make thy profit out of all occurrences; so shall every thing that happeneth unto thee be the source of praise.

The wise man maketh every thing the means of advantage; and with the same countenance beholdeth he all the faces of Fortune; he governeth the good, he conquereth the evil; he is unmoved in all.

Presume not in prosperity, neither despair in adversity: court not dangers, nor meanly fly from before them: dare to despise whatever will not remain with thee.—

Let not adversity tear off the wings of Hope; neither let Prosperity obscure the light of prudence.

He who despaireth of the end shall never attain unto it: and he who seeth not the pit shall perish therein.

He who calleth Prosperity his good: who hath said unto her, With thee will I establish my happiness; lo! he anchoreth his vessel in a bed of sand, which the return of the tide washeth away.

As the water that passeth from the mountains kisseth, in its way to the ocean, every field that bordereth the rivers: as it tarrieth not in any place: even so Fortune visiteth the sons of men: her motion is incessant, she will not stay; she is unstable as the winds, how then wilt thou hold her? when she kisseth thee thou art blessed; but behold as thou turnest to thank her, she is gone unto another.

SECTION II.

PAIN AND SICKNESS.

The sickness of the body affecteth even the soul: the one cannot be in health without the other.

Pain is of all ills that which is most felt: and it is that which from Nature hath the fewest remedies.

When thy constancy faileth thee, call in thy reason: when thy patience quitteth thee, call in thy hope.

To suffer, is a necessity entailed upon thy nature; wouldst thou that miracles should protect thee from it? or shalt thou repine because it happeneth unto thee? when lo! it happeneth unto all.

It is injustice to expect exception from that thou wert born unto: submit with modesty to the laws of thy condition.

Wouldst thou say to the seasons, pass not on lest I grow old? is it not better to suffer well that which thou canst not avoid?

Pain that endureth long is moderate; blush therefore to complain of it; that which is violent is short, behold thou seest the end of it

The body was created to be subservient to the soul: whilst thou afflicteth the soul for pain, behold thou settest the body above it.

As the wise afflicteth not himself because a thorn teareth his garment; so the patient grieveth not his soul, because that which covereth it is injured.

SECTION III.

DEATH.

As the production of the metal proveth the work of the alchymist: so is death the test of our lives: the essay which sheweth the standard of all our actions.

Wouldst thou judge of a life, examine the period of it; the end crowneth the attempt; and where dissimulation is no more, the truth appeareth.

He hath not spent his life ill who knoweth to die well; neither can he have lost all his time who employeth the last portion of it to his honour.

He was not born in vain who dieth as he ought: neither hath he lived unprofitably who dieth happily.

He that considereth he is to die is content

while he liveth; he who striveth to forget it hath no pleasure in any thing: his joy appeareth to him a jewel which he expecteth every moment he shall lose.

Wouldst thou learn to die nobly, let thy vices die before thee. Happy is he who endeth the business of his life before his death: who, when the hour cometh, hath nothing else to do but to die: who wisheth not delay, because he hath no longer use for time.

Avoid not death; for it is a weakness: fear it not, for thou understandest not what it is: all that thou certainly knowest is, that it putteth an end to thy sorrows.

Think not the longest life the happiest: that which is best employed doth man the most honour; himself shall rejoice after death in the advantages of it.

THIS IS THE COMPLETE

ECONOMY OF HUMAN LIFE.

FINIS.

CLOSING REFLECTIONS

Modern genetics confirms something the elders always knew: by the seventh to fourteenth generation, the clarity of our ancestral memory dissolves. Beyond that span, bloodlines braid and blur; identities we treat as fixed turn out to be shared, overlapping, and deeply intertwined. In truth, all of us walk with the same human inheritance. Whatever names or nations we claim today, our stories are related far more than we often admit.

It is from this posture of kinship—not accusation, not triumph—that this edition offers its final reflection.

The purpose of this work is not to discredit the communities who drew strength from *The Economy of Human Life* or its later incarnations. The meaning those communities created—the dignity, structure, hope, and identity they formed—deserves respect. Our people have always survived through myth, scripture, imagination, and improvisation. These tools carried us when empire, academia, and official archives did not.

But now, in 2025, the landscape has changed. We stand at a moment when classification, context, and intellectual transparency are not only possible but necessary. Our ancestors did not have worldwide manuscript databases, open-access translation tools, or a global digital library in every pocket. They worked with what they had. We now work with what we've been given.

This edition, therefore, comes not to correct the past, but to organize it; not to shame lineage, but to clarify it. We approach this text with generational grace while also acknowledging a modern reality: the same tools that grant us unprecedented access to knowledge also expose us to unprecedented misinformation. Scams, grifts, pseudo-scriptures, and metaphysical counterfeits proliferate faster today than in any century before—and far more convincingly. Discernment is no longer optional; it is spiritual self-defense.

This is why the charts, appendices, and timelines that follow are presented as both a map and a talisman. A talisman not in the occult sense, but in the ancestral one: a protective object that helps the seeker distinguish truth from trickery, wisdom from imitation, scripture from theatrics, and genuine lineage from opportunistic invention. In that sense, the correspondences that follow are a modern kind of amulet—knowledge organized as protection.

Proper categorization does not weaken belief; it stabilizes it. A tradition is stronger when it knows its sources. A seeker is safer when they know where a text comes from, who wrote it, and why. And a people are freer when they can tell the difference between revelation, reflection, and exploitation.

As you move through the comparative charts that follow—sacred canons, legitimate esoteric texts, repackaged works, historical forgeries, channeled visions, folk manuals—you will not find condemnation. Only context. Only classification. Only the quiet confidence that comes when you can name something correctly.

And so this closing ends with an invitation: not argument, not debate, but conversation. Let these pages encourage dialogue—between generations, between traditions, between the sacred and the scholarly mind. Let them help us speak more honestly about the texts that shaped us, the stories that misled us, and the wisdom that can now guide us forward.

> For we are all descendants of intertwined stories.
> Let us guard them—and one another—with grace and with clarity.

-Dennis Logan
The Honorable Scribe
Richmond, VA
December 6 2025

PSEUDO-ANCIENT SCRIPTURES WITH MODERN ORIGINS

Title (Date)	Claimed	Reality	Impact / Loss
The Aquarian Gospel of Jesus the Christ (1908)	Lost "missing years" of Jesus revealed from ancient records	New Thought pastor **Levi Dowling**, visionary composition	Influenced Moorish Science, New Age Jesus, yoga-Christian syncretism
Oahspe (1882)	Angelic dictation of cosmic history	Produced by a New York dentist (John Newbrough) in trance	Afro-American metaphysics, early New Age Bible, UFO & cosmic religions
The Book of Mormon (1830)	Ancient Hebrew-American plates translated by revelation	Blends KJV style, frontier theology, American folk motifs	Founded Mormonism (global religion), shaped American religious history
The Talmud of Jmmanuel (1970s)	Lost gospel revealing "real" Jesus as prophet Jmmanuel	Text tied to UFO contactee **Billy Meier**, modern fabrication	Alternative Jesus narratives in New Age / UFO circles
The Gospel of Barnabas (medieval; repopularized 20th c.)	Original gospel predicting Muhammad explicitly	Likely European creation with anachronisms	Used in Muslim apologetics, Afro-Islamic discourse, interfaith polemic
The Essene Gospel of Peace (1930s)	Essene manuscripts of Jesus teaching raw food & natural healing	Hungarian-origin pseudepigrapha, no known ancient manuscript	Influenced raw food, natural hygiene, New Age purity movements
The Book of Dagon (19th–20th c.)	Ancient Philistine scripture	Occultist fabrication drawing on biblical names & Lovecraftian aura	Occult Egyptomania, Cthulhu-era syncretism, fringe ceremonial magic
The Kolbrin Bible (1990s/2000s)	3,600-year-old Celtic-Egyptian Bible preserved in secret	Modern internet hoax blended with Theosophy & fringe history	Alternative-history circles, New Age prophecy, YouTube esoterica
The Sophia of Jesus Christ (misused, 20th–21st c.)	Literal historical teaching transcript of Jesus	Genuine 2nd–3rd c. Gnostic text, later repurposed as "lost words of Jesus"	Fuels modern Gnostic & esoteric Christianity; often misrepresented as canonical
The Gospel of the Holy Twelve (late 1800s)	Aramaic gospel promoting vegetarian Jesus	Victorian English forgery by Rev. Ouseley	Esoteric vegan Christianity, natural-healing & animal-rights spirituality

Title (Date)	Claimed	Reality	Impact / Loss
The Thunder: Perfect Mind (misrepresented)	First "feminine gospel" of historical Jesus movement	A Gnostic poetic text, not a canonical gospel	Becomes cornerstone for feminist theology, goddess-leaning metaphysics

REPUBLISHED KNOCKOFFS & REPACKAGED TEXTS

Title (Date)	Claimed	Reality	Impact / Loss
Hindu Magic (L. W. de Laurence, early 20th c.)	Ancient Hindu occult manual of Eastern sorcery	Recycled **Agrippa** + other Western grimoires with Hindu branding	Influenced Hoodoo, Jamaican Obeah, Black metaphysics; key mail-order text
Unto Thee I Grant (AMORC, 1925)	Tibetan wisdom text from hidden Masters	Recast of Dodsley's *Economy of Human Life* under "Sri Ramatherio"	Canon in Rosicrucianism; key bridge text for Moorish Science & Black metaphysics
Sixth & Seventh Books of Moses (18th–19th c. Germany)	Secret magical books of Moses	German folk-magic compilations stitched together and Hebraized	Foundational in Hoodoo, Obeah, African Christian magic and Bible-based sorcery
The Goetia / Lesser Key of Solomon (late Renaissance remix)	Solomon's personal demonology manual	Late Christian exorcism & magical texts reorganized under Solomonic name	Core text for Golden Dawn, Wicca, Afro-Caribbean ritual systems, modern occultism
"Egyptian Book of the Dead" (Budge editions, 1895)	Literal, authoritative translation of ancient funerary text	Highly inaccurate Victorian reconstructions & paraphrases	Shaped New Age Egyptology, Wicca, ceremonial magic; misinformed popular Egypt lore
The Book of Enoch (popular esoteric uses)	Ancient prophecy aligning exactly with UFOs, Nephilim conspiracies	Authentic Ethiopian text distorted by later occult & UFO interpreters	Fuels pseudo-angelology, Nephilim/alien narratives, fringe prophecy movements

Title (Date)	Claimed	Reality	Impact / Loss
The Book of Jasher (1840s American forgery)	Rediscovered Hebrew "lost book" cited in the Bible	Frontier-era forgery produced in the U.S.	Impact on Mormon folklore, fringe Judaism, Bible conspiracy cultures
The Book of the Law (1904)	Delivered by "Aiwass," an Egyptian praeter-human intelligence	Crowley's visionary trance text in Cairo	Foundational scripture for Thelema, chaos magick, later occult subcultures

CHANNELING, AUTOMATIC WRITING & "ASCENDED MASTER" TEXTS

Title (Date)	Claimed	Reality	Impact / Loss
A Course in Miracles (1975)	Direct dictation from Jesus correcting Christianity	Channeled by psychologist Helen Schucman in trance-like state	Major influence on New Thought, prosperity gospel, Oprah-era metaphysics
The Law of One / Ra Material (1980s)	Teachings of Egyptian god/entity Ra	Esoteric channeling sessions by a small group	New Age cosmology, "social memory complex," alien ascension doctrines
Conversations with God (1995)	Literal back-and-forth dialogue with God	Neale Donald Walsch's channeled/self-help text	1990s–2000s spiritual publishing boom; popular, non-dogmatic theism
The Urantia Book (1955)	Celestial revelation from super-mortal beings	Produced by Chicago circle with medical professional at center	UFO spirituality, cosmic New Age religion, complex angelology
Teachings of Ramtha (1980s–present)	35,000-year-old Lemurian warrior speaking through a channel	J.Z. Knight's trance-speech persona	New Age seminar industry; repeated accusations of cultic behavior
Seth Material (1960s–70s)	Interdimensional entity "Seth" teaching reality creation	Jane Roberts' automatic writing and trance sessions	Major seed for Law of Attraction, manifestation culture, modern metaphysics

Title (Date)	Claimed	Reality	Impact / Loss
Edgar Cayce Readings (1901–1945)	Akashic Records, Atlantean history, karmic diagnoses	Hypnotic trance readings of Cayce, interpreted by followers	New Age healing, reincarnation normalization, Atlantis obsession
Urantia "secondary works" (late 20th c. onward)	Follow-up celestial revelations expanding original Urantia	Community-generated material leveraging Urantia authority	Splinter sects, extended cosmic angelology, internal doctrinal fragmentation

PSEUDO-SCIENTIFIC SPIRITUAL TEXTS & OCCULT "SCIENCE"

Title (Date)	Claimed	Reality	Impact / Loss
The Secret Doctrine (1888)	Tibetan wisdom + ancient stanzas revealing root races	Blavatsky's synthetic cosmology, invented "Book of Dzyan"	Theosophy, New Age, racial spirituality; basis for root-race doctrine
Vril / The Coming Race (1871)	Hidden energy science of a subterranean super-race	Fiction presented in quasi-serious tone	Inspired Nazi occultism, "Vril energy" cults, modern energy mysticism
The Shaver Mystery (1940s pulp)	Ancient underground dero beings tormenting humanity	Fiction from a troubled author, later treated as "true"	UFO mythology, early conspiracy cosmology, Fortean lore
Worlds in Collision (1950)	Planetary catastrophes scientifically explain Bible events	Immanuel Velikovsky's pseudoscience	Catalyzed catastrophism cults, ancient aliens discourse, fringe cosmology
Chariots of the Gods (1968)	Ancient aliens built major civilizations	Fabricated archaeology, speculative "evidence"	Global pseudo-history, Ancient Aliens TV, mass-market alien mythology
Hollow Earth Texts (19th–20th c.)	Spiritual civilizations inside the Earth	Mix of fiction, fringe science, and occult speculation	UFO religions, New Age mythos about inner-earth masters & realms

POLITICAL OR CULTIC TEXTS WITH RELIGIOUS TONE

Title (Date)	Claimed	Reality	Impact / Loss
The Protocols of the Elders of Zion (early 1900s)	Blueprint of global Jewish conspiracy	Plagiarized political satire turned antisemitic forgery	Antisemitism, Nazi ideology, conspiracy culture **Loss:** fuel for pogroms & genocide
The Little Red Book (1964)	Sacred compilation of Mao's revolutionary wisdom	State-produced propaganda manual	Ritualized scripture in Maoist China **Loss:** Cultural Revolution violence & devastation
Heaven's Gate Doctrines (1990s)	Pathway to ascend to next evolutionary level via spacecraft	UFO religion developed by Applewhite & Nettles	End-times cult identity **Loss:** 39 confirmed dead in group suicide
The Turner Diaries (1978)	Prophetic, realistic vision of future race war	White supremacist fiction by William Pierce	Domestic terrorism blueprint (e.g., Oklahoma City)
Scientology's OT III Scriptures (1960s)	Hidden cosmic truth of Xenu and human trauma	Hubbard's sci-fi cosmology repackaged as religion	Billion-dollar religion; intense loyalty and controversy

ARCHAEOLOGICAL HOAXES WITH SPIRITUAL IMPACT

Title (Date)	Claimed	Reality	Impact / Loss
Piltdown Man (1912–1953)	Missing link early human ancestor	Fabricated fossil using human and ape bones	Misled anthropology; used in debates over evolution & human origins
James Ossuary (2002)	Burial box of James, brother of Jesus	Forged inscription on ancient ossuary	Millions spent, theological confusion, ongoing controversy
Shroud of Turin (14th c. forgery)	True burial cloth of Jesus bearing miraculous image	Medieval painted/treated cloth dated centuries after Jesus	Still venerated by millions; inspires devotion, apologetics, debates

Title (Date)	Claimed	Reality	Impact / Loss
Cardiff Giant (1869)	Petrified biblical giant discovered in New York	Carved gypsum hoax buried and "found"	Strengthened some literalist giant beliefs; famous cautionary tale
Mormon Kinderhook Plates (1843)	Ancient Native American record confirming Book of Mormon	Frontier forgers created hoax plates	Later embarrassment within LDS apologetics, used in critical scholarship

CULT LEADERS & FABRICATED SCRIPTURAL AUTHORITY

Title (Date)	Claimed	Reality	Impact / Loss
Father Divine's Parables & Doctrines (early–mid 20th c.)	Embodied God on earth delivering divine pronouncements	Charismatic leader with theological and social vision	Communal movements around racial equality & abundance **Loss:** property, autonomy, alleged abuses
Jim Jones' Red Book / Temple Sermons (1960s–1978)	Socialist-gospel revelation, prophetic guidance	Manipulative blend of Bible, Marxism, and personal control	Alternative Christian–Marxist experiment **Loss:** over 900 dead in Jonestown massacre
Koresh's "Seven Seals" (1990s)	Exclusive end-time revelation of Revelation's secrets	David Koresh's apocalyptic reinterpretation	Branch Davidian identity & siege theology **Loss:** 76 dead at Waco
Sun Myung Moon's Divine Principle (1957)	Completed testament clarifying Jesus' failed mission	Korean messianic reinterpretation by Moon	Unification Church (Moonies) global movement, strong group cohesion
Aum Shinrikyo "Mahāyogic Revelations" (1980s–1990s)	Final Buddhist-Hindu apocalyptic revelation for the last days	Shoko Asahara's hybrid apocalyptic system	High-control cult & terrorist group **Loss:** Tokyo subway sarin attack, multiple deaths

THEOSOPHICAL, OCCULT & ESOTERIC INVENTIONS

Title (Date)	Claimed	Reality	Impact / Loss
The Book of Dzyan (via Blavatsky, 1888)	Ancient Tibetan scripture older than all known texts	Invented / unseen text cited by Blavatsky	Root-race doctrine, cosmic cycles, New Age mythic scaffolding
The Mahatma Letters (1880s)	Astral letters from Tibetan adepts (Koot Hoomi, Morya, etc.)	Most likely forged/manipulated within Theosophical circles	Established Theosophical hierarchy and "Master" authority structure
Magic of India pamphlets (19th c.)	Ancient Indian magical manuals & secrets	Victorian occult propaganda using generic "Oriental" content	Orientalist esotericism, fueled Western fantasies of Indian magic
Rosicrucian Cosmo-Conception (1909)	Secret Western Mystery Science revealed from higher planes	Max Heindel's synthetic mystical system	Influenced occult fraternities, Theosophical splinter groups, esoteric astrology
Aquatic Apocryphon of Yada di Shi'ite (1930s pulp)	Ancient Lemurian priesthood manual	Occult pulp fabrication	Early UFO metaphysics, fringe Atlantis/Lemuria mythmaking

MODERN INTERNET-ERA SPIRITUAL HOAXES

Title (Date)	Claimed	Reality	Impact / Loss
Emerald Tablets of "Thoth" (2010s "translations")	Ancient Atlantean tablets by Thoth/Hermes	Modern New Age fantasy retro-attributed to antiquity	TikTok/YouTube esotericism, meme-ready quotes, Atlantean obsession
"Starseed" doctrines (2000s–present)	Human souls from other star systems incarnated on Earth	New Age reinterpretation of Theosophy, Ra, and UFO lore	Online spiritual communities, identity frameworks **Loss:** dissociation, identity confusion for some

Title (Date)	Claimed	Reality	Impact / Loss
QAnon "Q drops" (2017–present)	Cryptic divine-political revelations from insider prophets	Coordinated/chaotic internet LARP turned mass belief system	National movement, quasi-religion **Loss:** domestic terrorism, deaths, radicalization
"Law of Assumption" Neville misattributions (2020s)	Hidden Hermetic law newly revealed on social media	Viral remix of 1940s Neville Goddard lectures, often misquoted	TikTok manifestation religions, parasocial guru culture
Crystal Skull Prophecies (2000s–present)	Ancient Mayan/Atlantean artifacts with apocalyptic data	19th-c. European/German manufactured skulls	New Age prophecy culture, 2012-style apocalyptic myth cycles

FAKE AFRICAN, ASIAN & INDIGENOUS TEXTS

Title (Date)	Claimed	Reality	Impact / Loss
Stolen Legacy (1954)	Greeks stole all philosophy wholesale from Egypt	Deeply flawed historiography, but not malicious forgery	Afrocentric movements, Black cultural revival **Loss:** scholarly confusion, but positive pride outcomes
Nuwaubian "Right Knowledge" texts (late 20th c.)	Ancient Egyptian/Sumerian cosmic wisdom restored	Dr. Malachi York's invented cosmology	Esoteric Black nationalism, complex mythos **Loss:** cult abuse, criminal conviction
Book of Coming Forth by Day (fake "new" translations)	Secret Egyptian resurrection manuals recently recovered	Victorian mistranslations/creative editions sold as fresh scrolls	Afrocentric magic, New Age Egyptology, distorted Egyptian spirituality
Lemurian Scrolls (1930s–1960s)	Ancient Pacific priesthood records of lost continent	New Age fiction posing as rediscovered scripture	Neo-Pagan Pacific myth revivals, Lemurian lore, spiritual tourism

CHRONOLOGICAL TIMELINE (c. 1600–2025)

1. Early Modern Seed Stage (1600–1800)

Satire, Orientalism, and proto-hoaxes

- **1614–1617 – Rosicrucian Manifestos**
  Fama Fraternitatis, Confessio, Chymical Wedding published in Germany as a kind of mystical/political satire.
  → Later read as literal proof of an "Ancient Brotherhood," spawning real Rosicrucian orders.

- **1740s–1750s – The Economy of Human Life (Dodsley)**
  Anonymous English moral treatise presented as "translated from an ancient Brahmin manuscript."
  → Prints the template for fake Eastern scripture: short moral maxims + invented Asian backstory.

- **Late 18th c. – The Morals of Confucius & similar pseudo-Confucian texts**
  European attempts to package "Chinese wisdom" in Christianized, Enlightenment form.
  → Establishes genre of "Oriental wisdom" written by Europeans.

2. 19th Century: Romanticism, Spiritism & Pseudo-Scriptures (1800–1900)

- **1820s–1840s – Book of Mormon; Kinderhook Plates; Book of Jasher (American frontier)**
  Blended KJV language, local folklore, and forged "plates" to establish ancient American Israel.
  → Gives us a brand-new world religion (LDS) built on a mix of revelation, forgery, and sincere belief.

- **1840s–1870s – Spiritualist & Theosophical Forerunners**
  - Early **spirit communications** and "automatic writing" texts.

- Bulwer-Lytton's **Vril: The Coming Race** (1871) sold as half-serious "hidden energy" story.
  → Seeds for occult science, Nazi mysticism, later "energy" cults.
- **1882 – Oahspe**
  Dentist John Newbrough's voluminous "angelic dictation" of cosmic history.
  → Proto–New Age Bible; later sits on the same shelf as Aquarian Gospel, Urantia, etc.
- **1888 – Blavatsky's Secret Doctrine & Book of Dzyan**
  Claims to reveal ancient Tibetan stanzas and root-race doctrine.
  → Hardwires race-theosophy, ascended masters, and fake "Tibetan" lore into Western esotericism.
- **Mid–late 19th c. – 6th & 7th Books of Moses, grimoires, "Magic of India" pamphlets**
  German folk-magical texts repackaged as Mosaic and Hindu wisdom.
  → These become foundational in Hoodoo, Obeah, and African diasporic ritual systems.

3. Turn of the Century: Print-Boom & Occult Capitalism (1900–1930)

- **1908 – The Kybalion; The Aquarian Gospel of Jesus the Christ**
  - *Kybalion*: "Hermes Trismegistus" as cover for New Thought metaphysics.
  - *Aquarian Gospel*: channeled biography of Jesus with India/Egypt episodes.
  → Big influence on New Thought, New Age, and later on Noble Drew Ali.
- **1909 – A Course toward "Occult Modernity"**
  1909 Copyright Act in the U.S. formalizes the public-domain window.
  → Anything 19th c. or older becomes *free raw material* for occult publishers.
- **1910s–1920s – L.W. de Laurence in Chicago**

- Reprints grimoires, "Hindu Magic," and **Infinite Wisdom (1923)** — recycled Economy of Human Life with a Tibetan/Chinese backstory.
  ➔ His mail-order catalog becomes the de facto Black metaphysical library.
- **1923 – Infinite Wisdom (de Laurence)**
  ➔ Dodsley's moral tract reborn as "Tibetan secret doctrine."
  ➔ This is the bridge between 18th c. English moralism and 20th c. Black scripture.
- **1925 – Unto Thee I Grant (H. Spencer Lewis / AMORC)**
  Under pseudonym "Sri Ramatherio," Dodsley's text is reissued as Rosicrucian/Tibetan revelation.
  ➔ Canonized in AMORC's Rosicrucian Library.
- **1927 – Noble Drew Ali's Circle Seven Koran**
  Synthesizes:
  o Aquarian Gospel (Jesus chapters)
  o Unto Thee I Grant/Infinite Wisdom (moral chapters)
  o Theosophy/Oahspe-style cosmology
  ➔ Becomes foundational scripture for Moorish Science and, indirectly, NOI.

4. Mid-20th Century: UFOs, Cosmic Bibles & Apocalyptic Scripts (1930–1970)

- **1930s – Essene Gospel of Peace**
  Hungarian "translation" claiming Essene raw-food Jesus.
  ➔ Influential in natural-health and raw-food spiritualities.

- **1930s–1950s – Urantia Book**
  Chicago-based "celestial revelation" blending Bible, science, and cosmic hierarchy.
  → Proto–UFO religion, big impact on cosmic New Age thought.
- **1940s–1950s – Shaver Mystery, Hollow Earth, early UFO contactee literature**
  → Provide mythic skeleton for later alien-based spiritual movements.
- **1950s – Gardner's Wiccan Book of Shadows**
  Presented as ancient witchcraft tradition, but largely synthesized from older occult sources and his own invention.
  → Launches modern Wicca — a huge, living religious tradition built on a "forged" antiquity.

5. Late 20th Century: New Age, Self-Help & Weaponized Conspiracy (1970–2000)

- **1968 – Chariots of the Gods (Von Däniken)**
  Ancient aliens as civilizational architects.
  → Massive pop impact; seeds Ancient Aliens genre.
- **1970s – Talmud of Jmmanuel, Seth Material, Ramtha**
  "Lost Jesus gospel," entity channeling, Atlantean/Lemurian warlord gurus.
  → Alternative Jesuses, self-help metaphysics, New Age empowerment and confusion.
- **1975 – A Course in Miracles**
  Psychologist's inner dictation from "Jesus" becomes a global metaphysical text.
  → Filters into New Thought, prosperity gospel, Oprah-era spirituality.
- **1980s – Law of One / Ra Material**
  Channeled "social memory complex" teaching unity cosmology.
  → Influences serious esoteric circles online and in-person.

- **1950–1990s – Nation of Islam & related Afro-esoteric systems**
  - Foundational teachings implicitly downstream of: Economy of Human Life → Infinite Wisdom → Unto Thee I Grant → Circle 7.
  - Qur'anic base colored by Muhammad Ali's translation, anti-colonial rhetoric, and Afro-Asiatic identity.
    - → A mythic edifice combining scripture, pseudo-history, and real-world liberation impulse.

6. 21st Century: Internet Metaphysics, Meme Scripture & Viral Hoaxes (2000–2025)

- **2000s – Emerald Tablets of Thoth (modern "translations"), updated Atlantean lore**
  - → TikTok/YouTube "esoterica" using fake antiquity as content.
- **2000s–present – Starseed, Twin Flame, 5D Ascension doctrines**
  - Loose remix of Theosophy + Ra + New Thought.
    - → A new generation of "scriptures" born from clips and quote cards.
- **QAnon (2017–present)**
  - Political LARP becomes prophetic "scripture" for millions; Q-drops treated as sacred texts.
    - → Creates whole online ecosystems of identity and sometimes harm.
- **Social media era – Neville Goddard misquotes, Law of Assumption, manifestation cults**
  - 1940s lectures chopped, remixed, and sanctified as "lost Hermetic laws."
    - → Conspiracy religion becomes prophetic with real-world violence and deaths.
- **2025 – Your Edition of The Economy of Human Life**
  - First *honest* reissue situating the text in its full genealogical context:
  - Dodsley → de Laurence → AMORC → Moorish Science → NOI → Black esoteric culture.
    - → Turn from *hoaxing* to *healing* the lineage.

Editorial Notes for the Catalog & Timeline

On Faiths vs. Origin Stories

This catalog critiques *origin claims* and publishing histories, not the sincerity or worth of the communities that grew around these texts. A movement can be born from a forged, misattributed, or repackaged book and still produce real devotion, ethics, healing, and culture. Our goal is to clarify *how* these texts came to be labeled "ancient" or "revealed," not to discredit the people who found God, dignity, or direction through them.

On "Hoax," Imagination, and Channeling

Not every text listed here is a deliberate con. Many so-called "channeled" works arise from dreams, trance states, deep imagination, or psychological processes the authors themselves experienced as genuinely spiritual. In those cases, "hoax" would be too strong. What we are questioning is the *historical or archaeological* claims—"this is a 3,000-year-old manuscript," "this was written by ancient priests," "these plates came from an angel"—rather than the inner value readers may find in the ideas.

On Respect for Living Traditions

Some entries here sit at the very heart of living religions and esoteric orders. Listing them in this catalog is not a call to abandon those paths. It is an invitation to hold both truths at once: that a scripture's backstory may be modern, messy, or invented, and that people can still meet the Divine, heal trauma, and build just communities through it.

Provenance Still Matters

Honest provenance does not destroy faith; it matures it. By tracing how these texts travel—from satire to scripture, from pamphlet to canon—we honor the creativity of the communities who adopted them, especially Black, Indigenous, and colonized peoples who turned borrowed tools into instruments of survival and liberation.

NOTE ON THE FOLLOWING CHARTS

The pages ahead contain two parallel catalogs:

1. **Legitimate Sacred Texts** — the canons, scriptures, liturgical bodies, and oral traditions preserved through verifiable manuscript families, community transmission, and continuous religious practice.
2. **Legitimate Esoteric, Occult, Political, Philosophical, and Fraternal Texts** — works that shaped the modern mystical imagination, but did so *without false origin stories*, written by identifiable authors within known intellectual lineages.

These lists exist side by side for a reason.

The sacred canon anchors centuries of devotion, law, ethics, cosmology, and communal life.
The esoteric canon records humanity's experimental edges — the speculative, the symbolic, the visionary, the rebellious, the strange.

But the two bodies of literature require **discernment**.

Neither list is "hoax literature."
Both represent authentic human attempts to make meaning, whether through sanctioned priesthoods or solitary mystics.

Sacred texts are read as foundations.
Esoteric texts must be read as **interpretive, creative, or philosophical ventures**, not substitutes for scripture and not ancient revelations unless supported by history.

To help the reader navigate this terrain, a **Comparative Reading Checklist** follows — covering how to approach primary sources, how to identify pseudepigrapha vs. authentic manuscripts, how to weigh historical provenance, how to recognize hagiography, and how to maintain intellectual humility while exploring powerful symbolic systems.

Use these charts and the checklist together.

Not to elevate one tradition over another,
not to shame communities shaped by contested texts,
but to strengthen the reader's ability to distinguish:

- **What is canon**
- **What is commentary**
- **What is creative myth-making**
- **What is philosophical experiment**
- **What is later projection or invention**

—and to read *all* of it with clarity, curiosity, and respect.

GRAND CATALOG OF LEGITIMATE SACRED TEXTS

ABRAHAMIC — JUDAISM

Text / Collection	Time Period	Region	Provenance / Manuscript Lineage	Sect / Tradition
Torah / Pentateuch	1200–400 BCE	Ancient Israel	Masoretic Text; Dead Sea Scrolls; Septuagint	Rabbinic Judaism
Nevi'im & Ketuvim	800–200 BCE	Israel	Hebrew manuscripts; Qumran corpus	Rabbinic; Christian OT
Mishnah	c. 200 CE	Roman Judea	Codified Oral Law (Judah ha-Nasi)	Rabbinic Judaism
Talmud (Bavli & Yerushalmi)	3rd–6th c. CE	Babylonia/Judea	Rabbinic academies; strong manuscript families	Rabbinic Judaism
Midrashic Literature	2nd–10th c. CE	Israel/Babylonia	Rabbinic exegetical and homiletic tradition	Rabbinic Judaism

ABRAHAMIC — CHRISTIANITY

Text / Collection	Time Period	Region	Provenance / Manuscript Lineage	Sect / Tradition
New Testament (27 Books)	50–120 CE	Eastern Mediterranean	Thousands of Greek manuscripts; earliest papyri	Catholic, Orthodox, Protestant
Apostolic Fathers	90–150 CE	Mediterranean	Community-preserved early Christian writings	Proto-orthodox Christianity
Nicene & Ecumenical Creeds	325–787 CE	Roman Empire	Council acts; conciliar archives	Catholic & Eastern Orthodox
Philokalia & Orthodox Liturgies	4th–15th c.	Byzantine world	Monastic manuscript chains; liturgical books	Eastern Orthodox
Catholic Magisterial Texts	4th c.–present	Rome (global reach)	Ecclesiastical archives; papal bulls, encyclicals	Roman Catholic

ABRAHAMIC — ISLAM

Text / Collection	Time Period	Region	Provenance / Manuscript Lineage	Sect / Tradition
Qur'an	610–632 CE (compiled c. 650)	Arabia	Uthmanic codices; early manuscripts; oral hifz tradition	Sunni & Shi'a (core)
Hadith Collections	8th–9th c. CE	Arabia / Iraq	Isnād (chain-of-transmission) science	Sunni & Shi'a (different corpora)
Tafsir Literature	9th–14th c.	Islamic world	Classical exegetical manuscripts	All major Islamic schools
Fiqh / Islamic Law	8th–12th c.	Arabia–Persia	Legal treatises of Hanafi, Maliki, Shafi'i, Hanbali; Ja'fari	Sunni & Shi'a jurisprudence

EASTERN RELIGIONS — HINDUISM

Text / Collection	Time Period	Region	Provenance / Manuscript Lineage	Sect / Tradition
Vedas (Rig, Sama, Yajur, Atharva)	1500–500 BCE	India	Rigorous oral lineage; later Sanskrit śruti manuscripts	Pan-Hindu foundational canon
Upanishads	800–200 BCE	India	Sanskrit philosophical texts; multiple recensions	Vedanta
Bhagavad Gita	200 BCE–200 CE	India	Section of Mahabharata; stable manuscript families	Universal Hindu scripture
Puranas	300–1000 CE	India	Devotional Sanskrit anthologies, regional redactions	Vaishnava, Shaiva, Shakta

EASTERN RELIGIONS — BUDDHISM

Text / Collection	Time Period	Region	Provenance / Manuscript Lineage	Sect / Tradition
Pali Canon (Tipitaka)	1st c. BCE	Sri Lanka	Early palm-leaf manuscripts; monastic recitation	Theravada
Mahayana Sutras	1st–5th c. CE	India/China	Sanskrit originals, Chinese translations (Taishō canon)	Mahayana
Tibetan Canon (Kangyur/Tengyur)	14th c. redaction	Tibet	Monastic editorial redaction of sutras, tantras, śastras	Vajrayana (Tibetan)

EAST ASIAN RELIGIONS — CONFUCIANISM

Text / Collection	Time Period	Region	Provenance / Manuscript Lineage	Sect / Tradition
Five Classics	5th–3rd c. BCE	China	Imperial archival manuscripts; Han redactions	Classical Confucianism
Four Books (Analects, Mencius, Great Learning, Doctrine of the Mean)	4th–2nd c. BCE	China	Classical Chinese manuscripts; Neo-Confucian commentaries	Neo-Confucian canon

EAST ASIAN RELIGIONS — TAOISM

Text / Collection	Time Period	Region	Provenance / Manuscript Lineage	Sect / Tradition
Tao Te Ching	4th c. BCE	China	Bamboo manuscripts; Qin/Han editions	Taoism (philosophical & religious)
Zhuangzi	4th–3rd c. BCE	China	Classical Chinese manuscripts	Philosophical Taoism
Daozang (Taoist Canon)	5th–15th c. CE	China	Imperial woodblock collections; monastic editing	Religious Taoism

AFRICAN RELIGIOUS TEXTS

Text / Collection	Time Period	Region	Provenance / Manuscript Lineage	Sect / Tradition
Ge'ez Biblical Canon (Ethiopia)	1st–15th c. CE	Ethiopia	Ancient Ge'ez codices incl. Enoch, Jubilees, Meqabyan	Ethiopian Orthodox Tewahedo
Odu Ifá (Yoruba)	Centuries oral	Nigeria/Benin	Divination poetry; memorized odu corpus, later transcribed	Yoruba religion / Ifá
Pyramid Texts	c. 2400 BCE	Egypt	Tomb wall inscriptions in Old Kingdom pyramids	Old Kingdom Egyptian religion
Coffin Texts	2100–1600 BCE	Egypt	Coffin panels and tomb inscriptions	Middle Kingdom funerary corpus
Book of the Dead ("Coming Forth by Day")	1500–300 BCE	Egypt	Multiple papyrus scroll families; New Kingdom onward	New Kingdom Egyptian religion

INDIGENOUS TRADITIONS (AMERICAS)

Text / Collection	Time Period	Region	Provenance / Manuscript Lineage	Sect / Tradition
Diné Bahaneʼ (Navajo Creation)	Ancient oral	American Southwest	Oral narrative guarded by cultural stewards	Navajo religion
Great Law of Peace (Iroquois)	Pre-colonial	Northeast North America	Oral political–spiritual constitution; later written versions	Haudenosaunee Confederacy
Lakota Sacred Traditions	Ancient oral	North American Plains	Oral teachings; ritual songs and narratives	Lakota (Sioux)
Popol Vuh (Kʼicheʼ Maya)	Pre-colonial; ms 1701	Guatemala	Spanish-transcribed Kʼicheʼ text based on older oral tradition	Maya religion & cosmology

POLYNESIAN & PACIFIC TRADITIONS

Text / Collection	Time Period	Region	Provenance / Manuscript Lineage	Sect / Tradition
Kumulipo (Hawaiian Creation Chant)	Pre-contact	Hawaii	Oral royal genealogy/creation chant; later written down	Hawaiian religion
Polynesian Genealogies	Ancient oral	Tonga, Samoa, Pacific	Oral whakapapa and chiefly lines	Polynesian traditions
Māori Whakapapa & Karakia	Ancient oral	Aotearoa (NZ)	Genealogical recitations and ritual prayers	Māori spiritual practice

PERSIAN / CENTRAL ASIAN RELIGIONS

Text / Collection	Time Period	Region	Provenance / Manuscript Lineage	Sect / Tradition
Avesta	Oral (c. 1200–400 BCE); written 600–900 CE	Persia	Priestly oral transmission then Middle Persian manuscripts	Zoroastrianism
Pahlavi Texts (Bundahishn, Denkard, etc.)	3rd–9th c. CE	Persia	Sasanian and post-Sasanian religious scholarship	Zoroastrianism

GRECO-ROMAN & MYSTERY TRADITIONS

Text / Collection	Time Period	Region	Provenance / Manuscript Lineage	Sect / Tradition
Plato, Aristotle, Stoics, Plutarch	4th c. BCE–2nd c. CE	Greece/Rome	Greek and Latin manuscript traditions	Classical philosophy
Orphic Hymns	Hellenistic–Roman era	Greece	Hymnic papyri and later manuscripts	Orphic religious tradition
Mithraic Liturgy (overlaps PGM IV)	1st–4th c. CE	Roman Empire	Magical papyri; inscriptions	Mithraic mysteries
Eleusinian Hymns & Fragments	Classical–Hellenistic	Greece	Temple inscriptions; literary fragments	Eleusinian Mysteries

EARLY CHRISTIAN GNOSTIC (AUTHENTIC MANUSCRIPTS)

Text / Collection	Time Period	Region	Provenance / Manuscript Lineage	Sect / Tradition
Gospel of Thomas	2nd c. CE	Egypt	Nag Hammadi Coptic codex	Early Christian / Gnostic
Gospel of Philip	3rd c. CE	Egypt	Nag Hammadi library	Valentinian Gnostic
Gospel of Mary (Magdalene)	2nd c. CE	Egypt	Berlin Codex + fragments	Early Christian / Gnostic
Acts of Thomas	2nd–3rd c. CE	Syria	Syriac and Greek manuscripts	Syrian Christianity
Apocalypse of Peter	2nd c. CE	Egypt/Ethiopia	Akhmim fragment; Ethiopic copies	Early Christian apocalyptic

RENAISSANCE–EARLY MODERN MAGIC & OCCULT PHILOSOPHY

Text / Author	Time Period	Region	Provenance	Tradition / Influence
De Occulta Philosophia / Three Books of Occult Philosophy — Heinrich Cornelius Agrippa	c. 1510s (mss), 1533 (print)	Germany	Early Latin manuscripts and 1533 printed edition	Foundational Hermetic–Qabalistic magic; basis for Western ceremonial magic
De Vita Coelitus Comparanda — Marsilio Ficino	1489	Italy	Renaissance Latin treatise	Christian-Platonic astral magic; planetary talismans
Archidoxes of Magic — Paracelsus	1520s–1560s	Switzerland / German lands	Early medical–alchemical manuscripts; later prints	Spagyric medicine; proto-chemistry; occult healing
Paracelsian Medical Corpus	1520–1541	Europe	Autograph and student manuscripts	Reframed disease, spirit, and matter in early modern science
Monas Hieroglyphica — John Dee	1564	England	Printed hermetic–mathematical work	Symbolic synthesis of alchemy, Kabbalah, and astronomy
Spiritual Diaries & Enochian Records — John Dee	1581–1608	England	Latin/English manuscripts from scrying sessions	Enochian angelic magic; later Golden Dawn & Thelema foundations
Historia von D. Johann Fausten (Early Faust Book)	1587	Germany	Printed chapbook tradition	Birth of the Faust archetype; pact-with-the-devil mythos

EARLY MODERN GRIMOIRES & RITUAL MAGIC (AUTHENTIC MANUSCRIPTS)

Text	Time Period	Region	Provenance	Tradition / Influence
Arbatel de Magia Veterum	1575	Switzerland	Latin first edition	Christian theurgy, angelic magic, ethical occultism
The Book of Abramelin	14th–15th c. source, 17th c. mss	German-speaking Europe	Manuscript tradition	Holy Guardian Angel operation; crucial in Thelemic magick
Key of Solomon (Clavicula Salomonis)	14th–17th c.	Italy / Europe	Multiple Latin & vernacular manuscripts (Bodleian, BL)	Ritual circle magic; standard Solomonic toolkit

ANCIENT MAGIC CORPUS

Text	Time Period	Region	Provenance	Tradition / Influence
Greek Magical Papyri (PGM)	c. 100 BCE–400 CE	Roman Egypt	Actual papyrus manuscripts	Hybrid Greek–Egyptian temple magic; spells, exorcisms, theurgy
Mithras Liturgy (PGM IV)	2nd–3rd c. CE	Egypt	Segment of PGM	Mystery cult soteriology; ascent rituals
Orphic Gold Tablets	4th–2nd c. BCE	Greece / Magna Graecia	Funerary lamellae	Orphic afterlife instructions; soul-journey lore
Chaldean Oracles	2nd c. CE	Syria / Asia Minor	Fragmentary citations by Neoplatonists	Theurgic metaphysics; late antique Platonism

JEWISH MYSTICAL & MAGICAL CORPUS

Text	Time Period	Region	Provenance	Tradition / Influence
Sefer Yetzirah	3rd–6th c. CE	Palestine / Babylonia	Hebrew manuscripts	Proto-Kabbalistic cosmology; letters & sefirot
Sefer ha-Razim	3rd–6th c. CE	Late Antique Jewish world	Magical/angelic text; Geniza fragments	Angelic hierarchies, adjurations; Jewish ritual magic
Sefer Raziel ha-Malakh	13th c.	Ashkenaz (Germany)	Medieval Hebrew manuscripts	Practical Kabbalah, planetary and angelic operations
Hechalot & Merkavah Texts	1st–5th c. CE	Judea / Babylonia	Early mystical ascent literature	Throne mysticism; visionary journeys
The Testament of Solomon (Greek)	3rd–5th c. CE	Eastern Mediterranean	Greek manuscripts	Demonology; template for later Solomonic grimoires

ARABIC & ISLAMICATE ESOTERIC TEXTS

Text	Time Period	Region	Provenance	Tradition / Influence
Picatrix (Ghāyat al-Ḥikma)	10th–11th c.	Al-Andalus	Arabic mss → Latin translations	Astrological talismanic magic; essential medieval grimoire
Shams al-Maʿārif al-Kubrā — al-Būnī	13th c.	North Africa / Egypt	Arabic manuscripts	Sufi magic; Quranic letter & number mysticism
Ikhwān al-Ṣafāʾ (Epistles of the Brethren of Purity)	10th c.	Basra	Philosophical encyclopedic treatise	Esoteric Neoplatonism in Islamic frame
Magical & jinn narratives in Alf Layla wa-Layla (1001 Nights)	9th–14th c. compilation	Abbasid to Mamluk realms	Arabic manuscript tradition	Jinn lore; Islamic occult imaginary

FREEMASONIC, ROSICRUCIAN & FRATERNAL LITERATURE

Text / Body	Time Period	Region	Provenance	Tradition / Influence
Rosicrucian Manifestos (Fama, Confessio, Chymical Wedding)	1614–1617	Germany	Printed pamphlets	Sparked Rosicrucian mythos; Western esoteric orders
Rituals of Freemasonry (Blue Lodge, York, Scottish Rite)	18th–20th c.	Europe / Americas	Lodge archives; ritual monitors	Fraternal initiations; symbolic architecture of power
Morals and Dogma — Albert Pike	1871	USA	Scottish Rite publication	Masonic philosophy for high degrees
Secret Societies of All Ages & Countries — Charles W. Heckethorn / Mackenzie-type works	19th c.	UK / Europe	Encyclopedic reference books	Sourcebook for occult & fraternal lore
Rituals of the Hermetic Order of the Golden Dawn	1888–1903	UK	Cipher manuscripts, lodge papers	Modern ceremonial magic template (tarot, Enochian, Qabalah)
Israel Regardie – The Golden Dawn	1937–1940	UK/USA	Ex-lodge publication	Preserved Golden Dawn system; democratized access
Shriner & Prince Hall rituals (Afro-American fraternalism)	19th–20th c.	USA	Lodge ritual texts	Black fraternal and esoteric civic culture

OCCULT REVIVAL (19th–EARLY 20th c.)

Text / Author	Time Period	Region	Provenance	Tradition / Influence
Éliphas Lévi – Dogme et Rituel de la Haute Magie	1854–1856	France	Author-published	Father of modern ceremonial magic; Baphomet iconography
Éliphas Lévi – Histoire de la Magie (History of Magic)	1860	France	Printed work	Occult historiography; influences Blavatsky, Papus, Crowley
Isis Unveiled — H. P. Blavatsky	1877	USA	Two-volume theosophical work	Launch of Theosophy; syncretic occultism
The Secret Doctrine — Blavatsky	1888	India/UK	Major theosophical treatise	Root-race cosmology; huge imprint on New Age & esoteric racism
The Golden Bough — James G. Frazer	1890 (multi-edition)	UK	Anthropological study	Comparative myth/ritual; underpins "dying-and-rising god" narratives
The Rosicrucian Cosmo-Conception — Max Heindel	1909	USA	Rosicrucian text	Christian esotericism, occult physiology
Franz Bardon – Initiation Into Hermetics	1956	Czechoslovakia	Manual of graded practices	20th-century hermetic training bible

20th c. ESOTERIC, PROTO-SCIENCE & MODERN MAGIC

Text / Author	Time Period	Region	Provenance	Tradition / Influence
Rudolf Steiner – Knowledge of Higher Worlds	1904–1905	Austria	Anthroposophical lectures & text	Spiritual science; path-of-initiation manual
Rudolf Steiner – Occult Science	1910	Central Europe	Published treatise	Cosmology; esoteric Christianity
Manly P. Hall – The Secret Teachings of All Ages	1928	USA	Encyclopedic folio	Huge compendium of symbolism & esoteric traditions
Wilhelm Reich – Orgone writings (e.g., The Function of the Orgasm; Ether, God & Devil)	1930s–1950s	Germany/USA	Psychoanalytic + speculative science texts	Body, energy, repression; later counterculture icon
Peter J. Carroll – Liber Null & Psychonaut	1978	UK	Modern occult manifesto	Chaos magic, sigils, postmodern practice
Scott Cunningham – Wicca & herbal/magic manuals	1980s–1990s	USA	Practical guidebooks	Accessible neopagan/Wiccan praxis
Drunvalo Melchizedek – The Ancient Secret of the Flower of Life	1990s	USA	New Age series	Sacred geometry, merkaba lore

PRACTICAL MAGIC & FOLK RELIGION

Text	Time Period	Region	Provenance	Tradition / Influence
The Long Lost Friend — Johann George Hohman	1820	Pennsylvania (Deutsch)	German-American chapbook	Powwow/Braucherei, Christian folk magic
Roman Catholic Exorcism Rites (Rituale Romanum)	1614 → revised 20th c.	Rome	Official liturgical books	Institutional demonology and exorcism
Local grimoires & Braucherei notebooks (unnamed)	18th–20th c.	Europe / Americas	Handwritten family and village books	Everyday spell-craft, charms, blessings

LITERARY OCCULTISM & FICTION THAT BECAME "SOURCE TEXTS"

Text / Author	Time Period	Region	Provenance	Tradition / Influence
Goethe – Faust (Parts I & II)	1808–1832	Germany	Canonical literary drama	Alchemical, diabolical, Romantic quest myth
H. P. Lovecraft – Cthulhu Mythos corpus	1920s–1930s	USA	Pulp magazines, stories	Cosmic horror; "Necronomicon" meme; fed into modern occult aesthetics
Mikhail Bulgakov – The Master and Margarita	1930s (pub. 1967)	USSR	Satirical novel	Satan as trickster; esoteric Christianity and satire
Principia Discordia	1963	USA	Counterculture samizdat	Proto-chaos magic; Discordianism
Robert Anton Wilson & Shea – Illuminatus! Trilogy	1975	USA	Experimental novels	Conspiracy-as-mysticism; reality-tunnel culture

MODERN OCCULT MOVEMENTS & MANIFESTOS (LEGIT AUTHORSHIP)

Text / Author	Time Period	Region	Provenance	Tradition / Influence
The Book of the Law (Liber AL vel Legis) — Aleister Crowley	1904 (pub. later)	Egypt/UK	Crowley's holograph MS & typescripts	Thelema; "Do what thou wilt"
Magick in Theory and Practice — Crowley	1929–1930	UK	Thelemic treatise	Systematized his ceremonial magick
Liber 777 — Crowley	1909	UK	Tables of correspondences	Qabalistic cross-index of symbols
Anton LaVey – The Satanic Bible	1969	USA	Church of Satan publication	Modern LaVeyan Satanism
L. Ron Hubbard – Dianetics	1950	USA	Popular nonfiction	Foundation of Scientology
Lon Milo DuQuette – Enochian Vision Magick & other works	1990s–2000s	USA	Expository occult manuals	User-friendly Enochian & Thelemic commentary

BLACK POLITICAL, ESOTERIC & PAN-AFRICAN TEXTS (LEGITIMATE)

Text / Author	Time Period	Region	Provenance	Tradition / Influence
Marcus Garvey – Philosophy and Opinions of Marcus Garvey	1923–1925	Jamaica / USA	UNIA speeches & articles compiled	Pan-Africanism; Black nationalism; "Back to Africa"
Edward Blyden – Christianity, Islam and the Negro Race	1887	West Africa / Caribbean	Essays & lectures	Early Afro-Islamic and Afrocentric thought
Frantz Fanon – The Wretched of the Earth	1961	Algeria / France	Anti-colonial manifesto	Decolonization, revolutionary psychology
Cheikh Anta Diop – The African Origin of Civilization	1974	Senegal / France	Historical-philological study	Afrocentric re-reading of antiquity
Molefi Kete Asante – Afrocentricity	1980	USA	Philosophical work	Afrocentric paradigm in scholarship
Chancellor Williams – The Destruction of Black Civilization	1974	USA	Historical synthesis	Popular Afrocentric history; critique of empire & Christianity
Malcolm X – Speeches & The Autobiography of Malcolm X	1950s–1960s	USA	Recorded speeches and co-written autobiography	Black liberation theology, Nation of Islam to Sunni journey
Nana Asma'u – Islamic poetry & didactic works	19th c.	Sokoto Caliphate (Nigeria)	Fulfulde/Arabic manuscripts	Sufi women's scholarship; Islamic education networks
Amadou Bamba – Sufi writings	19th–20th c.	Senegal	Muridiyya manuscripts	Non-violent resistance, work-as-worship mysticism

PHILOSOPHY, POLITICAL THEORY & SOCIAL–ESOTERIC TEXTS

Text / Author	Time Period	Region	Provenance	Tradition / Influence
Sun Tzu – The Art of War	5th c. BCE (trad.)	China	Ancient bamboo & textual tradition	Strategy, power, later occult/leadership adaptation
Niccolò Machiavelli – The Prince	1532	Italy	Political treatise	Realpolitik, statecraft; favorite of occult "power" literature
Karl Marx & Friedrich Engels – The Communist Manifesto	1848	Germany	Political pamphlet	Revolutionary socialism; later occultized as "secular prophecy" by some
Friedrich Nietzsche – Thus Spoke Zarathustra	1883–1885	Germany	Philosophical novel	Prophetic style; will-to-power; huge shadow in esotericism
Carl Jung – Liber Novus (The Red Book)	1914–1930 (pub. 2009)	Switzerland	Illuminated private manuscript	Archetypes, active imagination; esoteric psychology
Anacalypsis — Godfrey Higgins	1836	UK	Antiquarian speculation	Early comparative religion; messy but influential on occult & Afrocentric streams

AFRICAN, INDIGENOUS & DIASPORA RELIGIOUS TEXTS (LEGITIMATE)

(These sit at the crossroads of "religion," "myth," and "magic," but with real provenance, not modern hoax.)

Text	Time Period	Region	Provenance	Tradition / Influence
Popol Vuh (K'iche' Maya)	16th–17th c. ms (pre-Columbian oral)	Guatemala	Colonial-era manuscript of older lore	Mayan cosmogony and myth
Odu Ifá Corpus	Precolonial–present	Yorubaland (Nigeria, Benin, Togo)	Oral divination verses, later transcribed	Ifá divination; Orisha theology
Kebra Nagast	14th c.	Ethiopia	Ge'ez manuscripts	Ethiopian Solomonic myth, Ethiopian Orthodoxy
Pyramid Texts, Coffin Texts, Book of the Dead	c. 2400–1100 BCE	Egypt	Tomb inscriptions, papyri	Core Egyptian funerary and magical corpus

Sacred Canon vs. Legitimate Esoteric vs. Hoax/Pseudo vs. Movements

SACRED CANON (LEGITIMATE)	LEGITIMATE ESOTERIC / OCCULT	HOAX / PSEUDO / REPURPOSED	MOVEMENTS & IMPACT
Torah / Prophets / Writings (Tanakh)	Sefer Yetzirah; Sefer ha-Razim; Sefer Raziel ha-Malakh; Merkavah/Hekhalot pamphlets	Sixth & Seventh Books of Moses; fake "Solomonic"	Jewish mysticism → Kabbalah → folk magic (Braucherei), Hoodoo, conjure
Psalms	Testament of Solomon (Greek)	Inflated demon catalogs; sensational exorcism manuals	Deliverance ministries, horror demonology culture
New Testament (Gospels, Letters, Revelation)	Apostolic Fathers; Philokalia; early mystics	Aquarian Gospel; Essene Gospel of Peace; Gospel of the Holy Twelve; Talmud of Jmmanuel	New Thought, New Age Jesus, Moorish Science (via Aquarian), alt-Christian movements
Qur'an; Hadith; Tafsir	Sufi writings (Nana Asma'u, Amadou Bamba)	Pseudo-Islamic "Moorish" genealogies; fabricated Asiatic histories	Moorish Science; early NOI framing; Afro-esoteric identity movements

SACRED CANON (LEGITIMATE)	LEGITIMATE ESOTERIC / OCCULT	HOAX / PSEUDO / REPURPOSED	MOVEMENTS & IMPACT
Vedas, Upanishads, Gita	Classical yoga commentaries; Vedanta; real Sanskrit schools	"Book of Dzyan," Ascended Masters, fabricated Atlantis/Lemuria lore	Theosophy; New Age; starseeds; crystal healing; 5D ascension
Buddhist Canons: Pali, Mahayana, Tibetan	Tantric commentaries; scholarly esoteric Buddhism	Urantia Book; Ra Material; Ramtha; Seth	New Age cosmology; law-of-attraction religion; channeling culture
Daoist Canon (Daozang)	Internal alchemy schools	Western Tao "secret texts" fabricated in the 1800s	Qigong cults; martial arts mythologies
Confucian Classics	Neo-Confucian metaphysics	Pseudo-Asian ethics books	Eastern-philosophy-for-white-audiences publication mills
Ge'ez Canon (incl. Enoch & Jubilees)	Kebra Nagast	Misattributed "Ethiopian secret gospels"	Rastafari, Afro-diasporic Ethiopianism
Odu Ifá; Yoruba Sacred Corpus	Authentic Ifá commentaries	"Egyptian-Moorish-Atlantean" synthesis texts	African esoteric revival; syncretic new religions
Egyptian Pyramid/Coffin Texts; Book of the Dead	Greek Magical Papyri (PGM)	Modern "Emerald Tablets of Thoth" (fabricated)	Occult Egyptomania; Hermetic revival
Gnostic Manuscripts (Thomas, Philip, Mary, etc.)	Hermetic corpus; Orphic tablets	Modern Gnostic fan-fiction gospels	Christ-consciousness spirituality; mystic psychology

SACRED CANON (LEGITIMATE)	LEGITIMATE ESOTERIC / OCCULT	HOAX / PSEUDO / REPURPOSED	MOVEMENTS & IMPACT
Indigenous Sacred Canons (Popol Vuh, Kumulipo, Great Law of Peace)	Anthropological commentaries	"Native American star-people scriptures" fabricated 1970–present	New Age appropriation; faux-shamanic movements
Zoroastrian Avesta & Pahlavi Texts	Late antique theurgic writings	"Lost Magian gospels"	Western occult Magian fantasy traditions
Classical Philosophy (Plato, Plotinus, Stoics)	Ficino; Agrippa; Paracelsus; Dee; Lévi	Occult pseudo-Platonism; Atlantis race doctrines	Western esotericism; ceremonial magic; Rosicrucianism
Christian Liturgical Rites (Rituale Romanum)	Authentic exorcism & demonology manuscripts	Sensational demon lists; Hollywood-driven grimoires	Paranormal media; deliverance subculture
Political Canons (Communist Manifesto; Destruction of Black Civilization; Garvey, Fanon, Diop)	Black liberation theology; Afrocentric scholarship	Protocols of Zion; Turner Diaries; QAnon	Real anti-colonial liberation vs. weaponized conspiracy religion
Wisdom Literature (Proverbs, Sirach, etc.)	Moral treatises; Stoic ethics	Economy of Human Life → Infinite Wisdom → Unto Thee I Grant → Circle 7 (hybrid)	Moorish identity; early NOI framework; Afro-Asiatic reorientation
Tibetan/Vajrayana Canon	Tantric manuals, commentaries	Fake Tibetan "Shambhala" scriptures	20th-century occult Tibet; mythic Asian origins

COMPARATIVE READING CHECKLIST

How to evaluate canon, apocrypha, hoaxes, and visionary texts with clarity—not confusion.

Use this checklist whenever you place two texts side-by-side: an authorized scripture and an unauthorized one, a canonical gospel and a pseudepigraphon, a historical account and a hagiography, a manuscript-rooted tradition and a modern "revelation."
This is how scholars, mystics, and responsible seekers guard the mind while studying the wide field of spiritual literature.

1. IDENTIFY THE GENRE BEFORE YOU READ

Every text tells you *how* it wishes to be read—if you listen.

- **Scripture:** community-preserved, manuscript-rooted, ritually transmitted
- **Apocrypha:** ancient texts outside the canon but still within the historical ecosystem
- **Pseudepigrapha:** writings falsely attributed to older figures (e.g., "Book of Enoch" traditions, 2 Baruch, Jubilees)
- **Hagiography:** idealized biography of a saint or hero, not strictly historical
- **Channeling / Automatic Writing:** imaginative or trance-produced content
- **New Revelation:** modern spiritual dictation claiming divine origin
- **Occult Manual / Grimoire:** ritual instruction, symbolic cosmology
- **Hoax / Fabrication:** intentionally deceptive or commercially motivated invention

Knowing the genre prevents you from reading poetry as history, allegory as doctrine, or fiction as revelation.

2. CHECK THE PROVENANCE

Ask the essential scholarly questions:

- **When did it appear?** (century, cultural setting)
- **Where was it found or first published?**
- **Are there manuscripts predating print?**
- **Who preserved it—one author, a sect, or an entire community?**
- **Was it anonymous? Misattributed? Claimed "ancient" without evidence?**

If the provenance is unclear or relies on miraculous discovery stories, read with heightened awareness.

3. EXAMINE ORIGINAL LANGUAGE & TRANSMISSION

A text's authenticity is often revealed by its linguistic fingerprints.

- Was it written in **the language of the era it claims**?
    - (Example: a "1st-century" text appearing first in Victorian English is a red flag.)
- Does it use **grammar, syntax, or vocabulary** inconsistent with its supposed age?
- Are there **multiple manuscript witnesses** or only one suspicious source?
- Has the text been **translated through several layers** (e.g., Aramaic → Greek → Latin → Victorian English → modern New Age remix)?

Where the language breaks, the illusion breaks.

4. IDENTIFY THE INTENDED AUDIENCE & SOCIAL CONTEXT

Every text serves someone.

Ask:

- **Who needed this text? Why now?**
- Was it written to:
    - console the oppressed?
    - build a new identity?
    - justify a leader's authority?
    - create exotic mystique for Western readers?
    - sell books during an occult or spiritual boom?
    - establish a religious hierarchy?
    - reform or revolt against existing structures?

Texts often reveal their purpose more clearly than their claims.

5. STUDY MOTIVATION & AUTHORIAL AGENDA

Discern whether the author is:

- **teaching**
- **explaining**
- **mythologizing**
- **prophesying**
- **selling**
- **leading**
- **controlling**
- **dreaming**

A text can be spiritually meaningful while still being historically unreliable. Not every author intends harm, but not every author intends truth either.

6. COMPARE THEMATIC CONSISTENCY WITH CANONICAL ROOTS

Ask:

- Does this text **align with**, **diverge from**, or **contradict** the established scriptural trajectory?
- Does it introduce:
    - historical impossibilities?
    - theological reversals?
    - anachronistic concepts (e.g., Victorian vegetarianism in a "1st-century gospel")?
    - sudden new cosmologies (e.g., Atlantis, Lemuria, space-brother angels)?
- Does it rewrite older tradition to *serve a new purpose*?

Contradiction itself is not disqualifying, but it reveals intention.

7. LOOK FOR RED FLAGS OF PSEUDEPIGRAPHA & FABRICATION

Common signs include:

- **Anonymity combined with ancient claims**
- **Sudden manuscript "discoveries" with no chain of custody**
- **Text appears first in modern English**
- **Exotic geographic claims unsupported by archaeology**
- **Overly perfect alignment with a new ideology**
- **Statements like "hidden for centuries until now"**
- **Blending multiple real sources without acknowledgment**
- **Using archaic language inaccurately ("thee," "thou")**
- **Claiming suppression by governments or scholars**

These do not automatically negate spiritual value—but they must inform interpretation.

8. IDENTIFY THE FUNCTION OF MYTH VS. HISTORY

Ask:

- Is this text trying to **explain a miracle**?
- **Fill a gap** in the known story?
- Give a community a **lost origin**?
- Address a **trauma or political absence**?
- Provide **rules, authority, or identity**?

Myth answers emotional and existential needs; history answers factual ones. Both matter—but differently.

9. WEIGH COMMUNITY RECEPTION

Authorized texts survive because **communities preserved them**, not because they fell from the sky.

Ask:

- Who copied this text for centuries?
- Who risked their lives for it?
- Who preached it, memorized it, chanted it, transmitted it?
- Did an entire tradition accept it—or only a single personality or small sect?

If a text has no communal transmission, it cannot function as communal scripture.

10. ASK THE FINAL QUESTION: WHAT DOES THIS TEXT *DO* TO YOU?

Not all value is historical.
Some texts are medicine; some are poison; some are mirrors.

Ask:

- Does it build humility or inflate ego?
- Does it create compassion or superiority?
- Does it ground you or detach you from reality?
- Does it call you deeper into your lineage or out of it entirely?
- Does it heal ancestral wounds or exploit them?

Impact matters.
A text can be historically false and spiritually beneficial.
A text can be historically true and spiritually harmful.

This is why comparison is essential:
truth is usually found between the lines, not inside a single book.

DEEP READING PROTOCOL

A structured method for evaluating sacred, pseudo-sacred, channeled, and questionable texts with intellectual clarity and spiritual responsibility.

This protocol teaches students to read slowly, consciously, and with discernment—honoring the living traditions behind genuine scriptures while responsibly engaging the creative, accidental, or manipulative inventions that orbit them.

Use this for ANY text: canon, apocrypha, channeled writing, grimoire, visionary literature, or cultural myth.

STAGE 1 — PREPARATION

1. Clarify Your Intent

Ask yourself:

- Why am I reading this text?
- Am I looking for history, theology, psychology, symbolism, or power?
- Do I want to understand the author—or use the author?

Set your purpose before you allow the text to shape you.

2. Identify the Genre

Before reading even one sentence, decide:

- Is this scripture?
- Apocrypha?
- Pseudepigrapha?
- Hagiography?
- Philosophy?
- Channeling?
- Fiction marketed as revelation?
- An occult manual or ritual text?

Never assume the genre the author claims is the genre the text actually belongs to.

STAGE 2 — CONTEXTUALIZATION

3. Establish Provenance

Ask:

- When?
- Where?
- By whom?
- In what language?
- Under what political, economic, or colonial pressures?
- Was there a community transmission or only one source?

A text without context can only be read as myth, not as history.

4. Map the Text's Lineage

Identify:

- Older texts the author copied, adapted, or contradicted
- Influences (e.g., Kabbalah, Vedas, Bible, Qur'an, Plato, Victorian occultism)
- Later traditions that adopted the text

Every text sits inside a long conversation.

STAGE 3 — CLOSE READING

5. Read the Structure

Look for:

- Recurring patterns
- Sections obviously borrowed from earlier works
- Sudden "breaks" revealing interpolations or later additions
- Ancient motifs awkwardly inserted into modern frameworks

6. Analyze the Language

Ask:

- Does the syntax match the period it claims?
- Are there anachronisms?
- Are "ancient" terms mistranslated or misused?
- Does the text imitate archaic English (thee, thou) incorrectly?

Language is the fingerprint of authenticity.

7. Identify Authorial Intention

A text often shows its purpose more clearly than its claims:

- To control?
- To unify?
- To inspire?
- To sell?
- To mystify?
- To empower?
- To deceive?
- To legitimate a leader?

Ask what the author *needs* from you.

STAGE 4 — COMPARISON

8. Compare Against Canonical Anchors

Look for:

- Doctrinal consistency or contradiction
- Historical plausibility
- Resemblance to other known pseudepigrapha
- Polemical rewriting of older stories
- Psychological projections or wish-fulfillment patterns

Comparison exposes what a text adds, removes, or distorts.

9. Track Theological Moves

Does the text:

- Expand the cosmology?
- Introduce new beings, realms, or magic systems?
- Reinterpret old stories with modern anxieties?
- Elevate a new authority figure?
- Create dependence on the author?

Every theological innovation has a motive.

STAGE 5 — IMPACT EVALUATION

10. Measure the Effect on the Reader

Ask:

- Does it provoke humility or superiority?
- Grounding or disassociation?
- Insight or confusion?
- Community or isolation?
- Compassion or contempt?
- Courage or paranoia?

Truth is what transforms—not what dazzles.

11. Evaluate the Social Function

Ask:

- Who benefits from this text's existence?
- Who is harmed or manipulated?
- When did this text emerge in relation to oppression, colonialism, or trauma?
- Was it created to provide identity, comfort, or control?

Texts are tools; tools can build or destroy.

STAGE 6 — SYNTHESIS

12. Ask the Final Question

"What is salvageable, and what must be left behind?"

Some texts should be embraced for their beauty, courage, and insight.
Others should be read as cultural artifacts, not spiritual guides.
A few should be quarantined as harmful mythologies.

But all can teach—if read correctly.

EXPANDED GLOSSARY OF TERMS FOR COMPARATIVE SCRIPTURE STUDY

Canon

The set of texts a religious community recognizes as authoritative.

Apocrypha

Ancient religious writings excluded from a community's canon but still historically valuable (e.g., 1–2 Maccabees, Wisdom of Solomon).

Pseudepigrapha

Texts falsely attributed to famous figures to gain authority (e.g., Enoch, Jubilees, Testament of Solomon).

Pseudepigraphon (singular)

A single work attributed to a fake ancient author.

Interpolation

A later addition inserted into an older text, often detectable through language or thematic inconsistency.

Redaction

The editorial shaping of a text—cutting, combining, arranging material to create a unified narrative.

Recension

A version or edition of a text with distinctive edits or alterations.

Hagiography

A biography of a saint that prioritizes spiritual message over historical accuracy.

Midrash

Jewish interpretive retellings that fill gaps, explain puzzles, or amplify themes in scripture.

Targum

Aramaic paraphrases of Hebrew scriptures—half translation, half interpretation.

Grimoire

A magical manual containing rituals, spells, invocations, and symbolic correspondences.

Mystical Literature

Symbolic, visionary, experiential texts describing encounters with the divine.

Gnosis

Spiritual knowledge understood as experiential, intuitive, or esoteric—not rational or institutional.

Revelation (capital-R)

A text presented as divine communication through prophets or angels.

Revelation (lowercase-r)

Personal insight, intuition, or visionary imagery interpreted as spiritually meaningful.

Automatic Writing

Writing produced during trance states, sometimes claimed to be dictated by spirits or higher beings.

Channeling

Mediumistic communication wherein a human claims to speak for spirit beings.

Heuristic Myth

A myth constructed not to deceive but to teach, heal, or illuminate spiritual truths poetically.

Forged Scripture

Text created intentionally to deceive or claim ancient authority.

Cultic Text

A writing used by a high-demand group to justify absolute authority, isolation, or obedience.

Orientalist Fabrication

European or American inventions falsely attributed to Eastern, Hindu, "Asiatic," or Egyptian sources.

Syncretic Text

A work combining multiple religious traditions, intentionally or accidentally.

Manuscript Tradition

The lineage of handwritten copies showing how a text evolved prior to the printing press.

Historical-Critical Method

A scholarly approach that analyzes a text by asking about its origins, audience, purpose, and historical context.

Hermeneutics

The art and method of interpretation—how we understand texts.

Textual Criticism

The science of comparing manuscripts to reconstruct the earliest attainable form of a text.

Mythopoeia

The deliberate creation of new mythology.

Esoteric

Knowledge intended for initiates, often symbolic or encoded.

Exoteric

Teachings intended for the broader public.

Provenance

The origin, authorship, and transmission history of a text.

Also Hear These Works in the Voice of Dennis Logan

Over the past decade I have devoted thousands of hours to recording sacred texts, apocrypha, and esoteric classics.

If **White Ancestors, Black Scripture** deepened your understanding,
you can continue the journey through our expanding library of works in scripture, apocrypha, esoterica, philosophy, folklore, mysticism, and political thought.

You will find many of the texts referenced in our Legitimate Sacred Texts Catalog,
our Legitimate Esoteric & Occult Corpus,
and even the works that inform our Grand Catalog of Hoaxes and Pseudepigrapha—all read, rendered, and reissued with care.

To explore the complete catalogue of **100+ audiobooks**,
from the Bible and Koran to grimoires, mystic treatises, revolutionary texts, and the great currents of world literature:

Search "Dennis Logan" on Audible.

New titles are released monthly as part of Penemue Media's ongoing commitment to clarity, preservation, and the restoration of our shared intellectual lineage.

Scripture, Apocrypha & Ancient Texts

- *The Universal Bible of the Protestant, Catholic, Orthodox, Ethiopic, Syriac, and Samaritan Church*
- *Lost Books of the Bible: The Great Rejected Texts*
- *The Book of Jasher*
- *Book of Enoch, Jubilees, Jasher & The Book of Giants: The Complete Scriptures of Nephilim & Fallen Angels*
- *The Books of Enoch and The Book of Giants (featuring 1, 2, and 3 Enoch with the Aramaic and Manichean Giants texts)*
- *The Book of Jubilees: The Little Genesis, The Apocalypse of Moses*
- *The First and Second Books of Adam and Eve*
- *The Pentautech: The 5 Books of Moses*
- *The War Scroll: The War of the Sons of Light Against the Sons of Darkness*
- *The Kebra Nagast: The Glory of the Kings*
- *The Book of the Bee: The Syriac Text*
- *The Holy Piby: The Blackman's Bible*
- *The Gospel of Nicodemus, the Acts of Pilate and the Harrowing of Hell*
- *The Books of Jasher*

Magick & Occult Classics

- *The Universal One: Walter Russell's Foundational Mind-Centered Electromagnetic Universe Treatise-Exact Facsimile with Full Illustrations*
- *Paradoxes of the Highest Science*
- *Aradia: The Gospel of the Witches*
- *The Magus or Celestial Intelligencer: A Modern Rendering of the 1801 Edition*
- *The Book of the Sacred Magic of Abramelin the Mage: A Modern Rendering of the 15th Century Grimoire*
- *The Lesser Key of Solomon: A Modern Rendering of the 17th Century Grimoire*
- *The Greater Key of Solomon: A Modern Rendering of the 15th Century Grimoire*
- *An Outline of Occult Science: A Modern Edition*
- *A Textbook of Theosophy*

Gnostic, Mystical & Esoteric Studies

- *Banned from the Bible*
- *The Secret Gospel of Mark*
- *The Gospel of Barnabas*
- *The Gospel of Judas: The Man, His History, His Story*
- *The Aquarian Gospel of Jesus the Christ*
- *The Gnostic Gospels of Philip, Mary Magdalene, and Thomas*
- *The Gnostic Scriptures*
- *An Advanced Lesson in Gnosticism*
- *The Apocryphon of John: A Gnostic Gospel*
- *The Secret Teachings of All Ages*
- *The Kybalion, Tablet of Hermes & Emerald Tablets*
- *Thought-Forms*
- *The Initiates of the Flame*
- *Golden Verses of Pythagoras & Other Pythagorean Fragments*
- *Science of Breath*
- *The Way of Initiation: How to Attain Knowledge of the Higher Worlds: A Modern Edition*
- *The Education of Children: From the Standpoint of Theosophy: A Modern Edition*

Original Works by Dennis Logan

- *The Panerotic Sutras of Master Stryfe*
- *The Apocatastasis of Enoch*
- *The Testament of Samson*
- *Try Satan: How One Man Outwitted the Devil, Misplaced His Wife, & Broke the Wheels of Fate*

www.ingramcontent.com/pod-product-compliance
Lightning Source LLC
Chambersburg PA
CBHW080433110426
42743CB00016B/3149